HEART TO TABLE

A Year of Cooking
for the People I Love

To Stephanie, ♡ Megan

MEGAN O'BLOCK

PHOTOGRAPHS BY
KRISTIN TEIG

FOOD STYLING BY
CATRINE KELTY

BOOK DESIGN BY
**ROBERT PARSONS/
SEVEN ELM**

FALL

WINTER

SPRING

SUMMER

INTRODUCTION

I was raised in an Italian-American family in New Jersey and the standards were very high for good Italian food. My mother, who was Irish, learned pretty quickly to become a good Italian cook. When I got married I was thrown into entertaining for my husband's office parties and boards that he served on. Being young and really inexperienced I found it daunting to say the least. Just as my mother had to quickly learn how to cook Italian food, I had to quickly learn how to throw a dinner party. I wish a book like this was available to me back then.

I decided to create this book to show how anyone can entertain at home and make it look easy. Entertaining can be easy—and here's the key—if you are organized. Throughout this book, I've created menus and included tips on what can be done in the days before guests arrive. I think people love gathering at my house because they enjoy being with friends and sharing meals, but also because they know how much I love the experience of hosting. I enjoy thinking about what dishes work well together and coming up with menus that my friends will like. I am well prepared, and on the day of the dinner party, I'm not stressed. There is nothing worse than guests seeing you sweat it out. Entertaining should be fun—and it is!

This book contains some of my most popular, tried-and-true menus. Each one takes into account diverse food preferences, the occasion, and the season. I'm a believer in seasonal cooking in the sense that sometimes in the colder months you feel like eating stews, but when the weather gets warmer you gravitate towards lighter meals—grilled fish and farm fresh vegetables eaten outside. All of the menus in the book, however, are interchangeable. If there's a salad that you like from the fall or winter menus, by all means serve it in spring or summer. Likewise, many of the recipes can be used in a variety of ways—soups that double as dips, sauces that can be added to pasta or spread on bruschetta. If you're taking the time to make something, it should last a few meals and a lot of these recipes work really well for that.

Here are some additional tips for throwing dinner parties:

MIX DINNER GUESTS / Conversations are much more interesting when everyone doesn't know one another. I used to do fancier parties in the dining room with place cards but now I just have a rough idea of who should sit next to whom and I'll suggest it. I think people appreciate being told where to sit. Even if we are eating casually, I have couples split up and always do boy-girl-boy-girl around the table.

CREATE A MUSIC PLAYLIST / Each of the menus in this book has a suggested music playlist, which I've created with the help of family and friends and posted to Spotify. Music is important during a party. While I cook—barefoot in my kitchen, always—I'm listening to loud music, and my tastes are all over the place. I can go from The Rolling Stones to Ella Fitzgerald to Camille Saint-Saëns. I hope the playlists inspire you to listen and discover new music.

PAIR YOUR WINE / I am lucky to have a good friend in Carmine Martignetti, the preeminent liquor distributor in our area. He and his highly educated staff have made wine pairing suggestions for each of the menus in the book, taking into consideration the acidity in foods and how it impacts how wine will taste. Best of all, these wines are reasonably priced.

CREATE TABLE SETTINGS / Years ago, I started collecting miniature vases. Now, for holidays my husband and three sons will give me a new one. These vases make it easy when I am setting the table for dinner: each vase gets a single stem and each guest seat gets a vase. I also always use candles. Even when my boys were in grade school, I put candles on the table every night for dinner. As they got older, it was a big deal for them to light the candles. I remember once a friend dropped something off just before dinner. When she saw the table set with linens and candles, she asked if I was having company. She was shocked when I told her that I set the table for dinner that way every night. Mealtime was always important to me. I loved having my family gathered around the table and hearing about their day. As a result, my sons are magnificent conversationalists. That's something I'm very proud of.

IF GUESTS OFFER TO BRING SOMETHING, LET THEM / If guests offer to bring wine, ask them to bring two bottles of the same wine. Another good item to bring is a tossed salad, but say you'll make the dressing. Dessert is an easy thing to bring as well. In Italy, guests are known to swing by a good Italian bakery and pick up a tray of butter cookies, cannoli, or pastries. Guests feel good about helping out and that leaves less for you to do.

MOVE AROUND FOR DESSERT / By the time dessert rolls around, it's nice to be able to get up from your seat. Sometimes you've exhausted your conversation with the two people next to you. One reason I like serving cookies is because they're easy and mobile. They're also smaller portions. So many guests these days are watching their weight or avoiding sugar. You will see from my menus that I also provide fruit for those who prefer no sugar.

ASK ABOUT FOOD LIMITATIONS / More and more guests have limitations these days—gluten or dairy or other allergies, or they're abstaining from sugar or grains or whatnot. When sending invitations, always ask guests if they have any food allergies or preferences. I try very hard to please all my guests and to respect their life choices.

RENT EQUIPMENT / I've been known to rent equipment—simple white dishes, wine glasses, flatware, and other items—when I'm entertaining more than 10 people. The cost is not exorbitant, they deliver and pick up, and you don't have to wash them! You simply rinse and put them back in the bins the company provides. I've also hired help if my numbers are higher than 10, which can also reduce stress.

SEND HOME DOGGIE BAGS / As I was working on this book, I'd send guests home with the recipes of what we'd eaten as well as "doggie bags." If they were so inclined, I'd ask them to test my recipes and send along any thoughts or feedback, all of which have been incorporated into the final recipes. I encourage you to have containers available for your guests to take home food from your party. They are so appreciative and it's the equivalent of a grown up goodie bag!

Once while having dinner at a restaurant with another couple, the wife asked me how many nights I cook for my husband. I think she was shocked to hear the answer, which is almost every night. Quite frankly, her husband looked jealous. My husband dislikes eating out and whenever we do he sometimes says, "You make this better." What he doesn't understand is that I like to dress up once in a while and put my high heels on! But I can't deny that I'm happiest barefoot and listening to loud music while cooking in my kitchen. I love the creative outlet that cooking provides me, I love the smell of my kitchen while I'm cooking, and it may sound old-fashioned, but I love the satisfaction of knowing I'm feeding the people I love.

I hope you enjoy my new cookbook.

FALL

HEART TO TABLE

» I enjoy having friends and family come over on a Sunday for a big buffet, and everybody loves Italian food. I get such joy from watching different groups gather in different parts of my kitchen and family room. This menu is filled with dishes that make people happy, and they're easy to execute. You can make many of the recipes in advance, and I've included items on the buffet table that can be bought as well. I encourage you to throw a party like this. Your friends will appreciate being invited.

ITALIAN BUFFET

MENU

COLD ANTIPASTO

Olives

Cabbage and Portobello
Mushroom Salad

HOT ANTIPASTO

Adriatic Shrimp

Stuffed Mushrooms
with Béchamel

BUFFET TABLE

My Mom's Lasagna

Baked Eggplant

Italian Bread

Green Salad with
White Wine Vinaigrette
and Oregano

DESSERT TABLE

Torta Della Nonna

Cannoli

Clementines

WINE

REDS / 2014 Tenuta Sant'Antonio
Scaia Corvino (Veneto, Italy)

2014 Ascheri Barbera d'Alba
'Fontanelle' (Piedmont, Italy)

WHITES / 2014 Bortoluzzi Pinot
Grigio (Friulli, Italy)

2014 Batasiolo Gavi di Gavi
'Granee' (Piedmont, Italy)

ENTERTAINING NOTES

3 DAYS BEFORE / Set table. Prepare playlist. Choose and purchase wine. Place stick'ems on bowls and platters. Food shop (including meat but not shrimp). Buy flowers. Make huge pot of Fuggedaboutit Tomato Gravy for eggplant and lasagna.

2 DAYS BEFORE / Make Torta Della Nonna (make two if having more than eight people). Make vinaigrette. Make mustard dip.

1 DAY BEFORE / Buy shrimp. Buy cannoli and Italian bread. Make Baked Eggplant (two trays if having more than eight people), My Mom's Lasagna (one to two without sausage and one to two with sausage), Cabbage and Mushroom Salad, and Stuffed Mushrooms. Clean lettuce and put in Ziploc bag.

DAY OF DINNER / Remove from refrigerator Baked Eggplant, My Mom's Lasagnas, Stuffed Mushrooms, and mustard dip. Make shrimp.

JUST BEFORE GUESTS ARRIVE / One hour before guests arrive, preheat oven to 350 degrees. 30 minutes before guests arrive, place Baked Eggplant, My Mom's Lasagnas, and Stuffed Mushrooms in oven, covered tightly in tin foil.

WHEN GUESTS ARRIVE / Put out cold and hot antipasto dishes. After reheating hot dishes, remove from oven and place on buffet table. Toss salad and put out. Cut and put out Italian bread. After main course is finished, put out desserts.

PLAYLIST

Fly Me to the Moon Frank Sinatra / **Mambo Italiano** Rosemary Clooney / **Somethin' Stupid** Nancy Sinatra and Frank Sinatra / **Mean and Evil Blues** Dinah Washington / **You Send Me** Sam Cooke / **Love You Most of All** Sam Cooke / **Having a Party** Sam Cooke / **Mama's Pearl** Jackson 5 / **Reach Out** Mad Satta / **If I Could Build My Whole World Around You** Marvin Gaye / **I Heard It Through the Grapevine** Marvin Gaye / **You Made Me Love You** Harry James / **The Way You Look Tonight** Frank Sinatra / **That's Life** Frank Sinatra / **My Way** Frank Sinatra / **L-O-V-E** Nat King Cole / **Vieni Su (Say You Love Me Too)** Dean Martin / **Take Me in Your Arms (Torna a Surriento)** Dean Martin / **It's Impossible** Perry Como / **Tu Vou' Fa L'Americano** Fiorello, Matt Damon, and Jude Law / **My Funny Valentine** Matt Damon / **Italia** Harry Rabinowitz / **O Mio Babbino Caro from Gianni Schicchi** Puccini / **The Godfather Waltz** Nino Rota / **Love Theme from The Godfather** Nino Rota

1 HOUR, 12 MINUTES; PLAYLIST AND SONGS AVAILABLE ON SPOTIFY (MEGANOBLOCK)

CABBAGE AND PORTOBELLO MUSHROOM SALAD

Many restaurants in Italy feature a table at the front containing a variety of cold antipasti. I like to recreate this table at home. This particular dish is a healthy choice to include.

Serves: 4

½ green cabbage,
   cored and thinly sliced

3 portobello mushrooms,
   thinly sliced

4 tablespoons olive oil
   (more if necessary)

   Juice of 2 lemons

   Kosher salt and
   freshly ground pepper

   Parmesan cheese, shaved
   (use vegetable peeler)

1 In a bowl, toss cabbage and mushrooms with olive oil, lemon juice, and salt and pepper to taste. Let stand for up to 30 minutes. Taste and correct for seasoning, adding more olive oil if necessary.

2 Top with shaved Parmesan cheese before serving.

ADRIATIC SHRIMP

If I offer to bring a dish to a dinner party or a book club meeting, I bring these shrimp. They also work well as part of your table of antipasti. They are easy to make and taste nice served warm or at room temperature.

Serves: 8

SHRIMP

24	uncooked shrimp, peeled and deveined
4	tablespoons olive oil
4	tablespoons canola oil
1	cup Italian breadcrumbs
1	garlic clove, chopped finely
3	teaspoons fresh Italian flat leaf parsley, chopped finely
	Kosher salt and freshly ground pepper
	Lemon wedges

MUSTARD DIP

½	cup Dijon mustard
4	tablespoons Grapeseed oil
	Juice of 1 lemon
	Kosher salt and freshly ground pepper

1 FOR THE SHRIMP: Preheat oven on Broil (you could also cook these on an outdoor grill).

2 After cleaning your shrimp, dry them thoroughly on paper towels. This is very important. If you don't dry them enough, the breadcrumbs become mushy. Toss the shrimp with the oils, breadcrumbs, garlic, and parsley, and salt and pepper to taste. Let sit for 20 minutes at room temperature.

3 Place shrimp under broiler or on grill and cook approximately 2 minutes each side, until golden. Serve with lemon wedges and homemade mustard dip.

4 FOR THE MUSTARD DIP: Mix all ingredients together. Serve.

STUFFED MUSHROOMS WITH BÉCHAMEL

This is a crowd pleaser. I don't know anyone that doesn't love stuffed mushrooms. Also, these will make your kitchen smell fantastic!

Serves: 8

MUSHROOMS

- 36 small to medium white or cremini mushrooms
- 2½ tablespoons salted butter
- 1 shallot, chopped (approximately 1 tablespoon)
- 3 slices of prosciutto, fat removed and chopped (approximately 3 tablespoons)

  Kosher salt and freshly ground pepper
- 2 tablespoons Italian breadcrumbs

BÉCHAMEL

- 1 cup of milk
- 2 tablespoons flour
- 1½ tablespoons salted butter
- 3 tablespoons grated Parmesan cheese

  Kosher salt to taste (Parmesan is salty, so you may find you don't need)

1 You'll need a 9″ x 13″ baking dish. Preheat oven to 450 degrees.

2 FOR THE MUSHROOMS: Wipe the mushrooms clean with damp paper towels (you will go through many). Detach stems and chop them, leaving cap of mushroom whole.

3 Sauté shallots over medium heat in butter until golden, approximately 3 minutes. Add prosciutto and continue to sauté, approximately 1 to 2 minutes. Add chopped mushroom stems, salt and pepper to taste, and continue to sauté, stirring often, approximately 2 to 3 minutes more. Set aside.

4 FOR THE BÉCHAMEL: Warm the milk over low heat in a small pot or microwave. In a separate small pot, mix flour and butter, and cook over low heat until butter is melted and a paste forms. Slowly add milk a little at a time while whisking.

5 Add salt (if using) and cheese and continually whisk until it's a creamy consistency.

6 Add mushroom mixture to the warm béchamel. Add a little more Parmesan cheese to taste. Stir to combine.

7 Place the mushroom caps hollow side up in a butter-smeared baking dish. Fill with the béchamel stuffing, and sprinkle with breadcrumbs.

8 Bake for 15 minutes or until golden. Can be made one day in advance. Keep covered in refrigerator until ready to serve. Reheat at 450 degrees for approximately 15 minutes. Serve hot.

VINAIGRETTE

Change up your salads and you will never tire of having one each night. Use a variety of vinegars and herbs. Add shaved carrots, radishes, cucumbers, and tomatoes in season. You can even get fancy and add edible flowers!

One thing I ask: Promise me you won't buy grocery store salad dressing. (As my father would say, "That's real shit.") Do you ever wonder why it can stay on the shelf for so long? It's loaded with salt! If you make a batch of dressing on the weekend, it should last you all week long.

Serves: 4

1   tablespoon Dijon mustard

2   tablespoons vinegar
     (red wine, white wine, sherry,
     raspberry, or balsamic)

¼   cup olive oil

     Juice of 1 lemon

     Kosher salt and
     freshly ground pepper

OPTIONAL ADD-INS

1   tablespoon honey

     Fresh or dried herbs, like
     Herbs de Provence, oregano,
     Italian seasoning

     For a Caesar salad:
     freshly grated Parmesan
     cheese and 1 tablespoon
     Red Boat Fish Sauce
     (find it on Amazon.com),
     which adds a saltiness
     without using anchovies.

1   Combine all ingredients and whisk until thick, or put into a sealed container and shake.

A NOTE ON INGREDIENTS

The key to a good salad is to use the very best ingredients. To start, please buy extra virgin olive oil. I prefer olive oil from Tuscany but everyone has his or her own preference—I encourage you to experiment. Once, I stopped into a little Italian grocery in Boston's North End and met an old lady who talked my head off about the olive oil of Puglia and how she felt it was the best! Naturally, in front of her I had to purchase some and besides, my father's mother was from Bari, the capital of Puglia. So I thought I'd give it a try. It was lighter than I prefer, though for my Arugula Pesto it works nicely. The lesson: Experiment and see what your family and friends prefer.

If you are using balsamic vinegar, I suggest you "splurge" on a really high quality one made for salads. The Modena region makes the best. Modena is also where Ferraris are manufactured. As I like to tell my three sons, "If you ever visit Modena you can buy yourself a Ferrari, but bring your mother back some balsamic vinegar." If you are making a recipe in which the vinegar will be cooked and reduced, like the Grilled Vegetables with Balsamic Syrup (page 116) and Grilled Peaches (page 122), then it's perfectly okay to use a cheaper version.

If you don't already own a pepper mill, go out right now and buy one. You will taste a huge difference in your dishes after you have tried freshly ground pepper. I like to buy the bags of peppercorns that include a variety of colors—white, green, red, and black—all together.

Lastly, I know salt is not good for you, but a little in a salad goes a long way. I only use Kosher salt—never table salt. Iodized salt should only be used for baking.

FUGGEDABOUTIT TOMATO GRAVY

Growing up in New Jersey with an Italian father, we called tomato sauce "gravy." I have such fond memories of waking up on the weekend to the smell of garlic and olive oil. Sometimes my father made it without any meat (marinara), and sometimes he made it with a mix of hot and sweet sausages or meatballs. He would fry up meatballs and hand one to me on a fork. I'd take it into the living room to eat while watching cartoons. I still prefer my meatballs without gravy. My father usually used garlic but occasionally, especially in the summer, he used onions in his sauce. I find onions often disagree with people, so I rarely cook with them.

Since there are only a few ingredients in gravy, quality is very important. Use only fresh garlic, really good extra virgin olive oil, and San Marzano Italian peeled tomatoes. When buying tomatoes, look for DOP, which stands for the Italian phrase Denominazione d' Origine Protetta (roughly, "protected designation of origin").

The recipe below is for classic gravy, which can be customized according to your personal tastes—you can add meatballs, sausage, or pork, for instance, or red pepper flakes for an Arrabbiata. Serve with penne or your favorite pasta. I usually triple the recipe as this gravy lasts one week in your refrigerator or months in your freezer. Friends and neighbors love this stuff!

Serves: 6 to 8

¼ cup olive oil

6 garlic cloves, crushed

1 28-ounce can San Marzano whole peeled plum tomatoes, blended

1 6-ounce can tomato paste

Herbs to taste. Dry or fresh, but if using fresh, you'll need more.*

Kosher salt and freshly ground pepper

1 Add olive oil and crushed garlic to a large pot and sauté over medium heat for approximately 1 to 2 minutes, being careful not to burn. Add blended tomatoes to the pot and stir to combine. Cook over medium heat for about 10 minutes.

2 Add tomato paste and herbs and salt and pepper to the pot. If after adding paste you think it's too thick, just add a little water.

3 Lower heat. Cook uncovered for about 20 minutes. If you're adding meatballs or sausages, fry them a little, pat on paper towels, then add to gravy for 30 minutes.

4 Taste and correct for seasoning. Serve with your favorite pasta or use in any tomato sauce-based dish.

A NOTE ON HERBS

*Herbs are a great way to make gravy yours. Some like a basil and parsley combination. Those with spicier tastes might like oregano and crushed red pepper. My family likes a parsley/basil blend, and so for the above recipe I'll usually do ½ tablespoon dried parsley and 1 tablespoon dried basil.

MY MOM'S LASAGNA

Though my mother was Irish, marrying an Italian man from Hoboken meant that she had to learn to cook Italian food. She made really good lasagna. For Thanksgiving, we always had this lasagna as an option along with the traditional, boring (in my opinion) turkey.

Serves: 8 to 12

1-2   boxes of precooked
      lasagna sheets

2   quarts of Fuggedaboutit
    Tomato Gravy*

32   ounces (2 pounds)
     whole milk ricotta

2   eggs, beaten

¼   cup fresh Italian flat
    leaf parsley, chopped,
    plus some for top

2-3   teaspoons Parmesan
      cheese, grated

      Kosher salt and
      freshly ground pepper

2-3   balls of fresh mozzarella
      cheese, chopped (2½ cups)

1   You'll need a 9″ x 13″ baking dish. Preheat oven to 350 degrees.

2   In a large bowl, mix ricotta, beaten eggs, parsley, Parmesan cheese and some salt and pepper. Chop mozzarella cheese.

3   Spread a layer of gravy on the bottom of baking dish. Place lasagna sheets on top, then a layer of the ricotta mixture, followed by a sprinkle of mozzarella and another layer of gravy. Repeat these steps 2 to 3 times to the top of the baking dish, ending with gravy. Sprinkle parsley and Parmesan cheese on top.

4   Cover tightly with tin foil. Bake for 30 to 40 minutes. Can and should be made one day in advance. Store covered in refrigerator until ready to serve. Reheat covered in tin foil at 350 degrees for 45 minutes. Have extra gravy for guests to add to their plates.

A NOTE ON GRAVY

*If you want sausages in your lasagna, add sautéed sausages to the gravy and cook another 30 minutes. When ready to assemble the lasagna, remove the sausages and add layers of sliced sausages in between the ricotta and mozzarella.

BAKED EGGPLANT

I used to bread and fry my eggplant, but it's time consuming, not as healthy, and quite frankly, I now prefer this version.

Serves: 6

1 quart Fuggedaboutit Tomato Gravy

2 medium eggplants, peeled

Unsalted butter (or olive oil)

Parmesan cheese, grated

Fresh mozzarella (optional)

Freshly ground pepper

1 You'll need a 9″ x 13″ baking dish. Preheat oven to 350 degrees.

2 Slice peeled eggplant thin on the long edge, then lay flat on paper towels on the counter. Cover the slices with Kosher salt and wait 5 to 10 minutes. Wipe away the "sweat" from the surface of the slices, flip, salt, and repeat.

3 Sauté eggplant slices in butter or spread olive oil on both sides and bake in 350 degree oven. Bake approximately 5 to 10 minutes each side, until soft but not mushy.

4 Spread a layer of gravy on the bottom of a baking dish. Arrange a layer of eggplant, then a layer of gravy. Sprinkle with grated Parmesan cheese, then add another layer of eggplant, then gravy, then cheese, for up to three layers. Sprinkle top with pepper to taste.

OPTIONAL: You may opt to finish with a layer of thinly sliced mozzarella cheese.

5 Place in oven to brown for approximately 30 minutes. Can and should be made one day in advance. Keep covered in refrigerator until ready to serve. Reheat at 350 degrees for approximately 20 minutes. Serve hot.

GRAVY, GRAVY, AND MORE GRAVY

Freezer Staple / The Fuggedaboutit Tomato Gravy recipe is used for all of the tomato-based dishes in this book: My Mom's Lasagna (page 22) and Cod with Fuggedaboutit Tomato Gravy (page 104). I also use it when making Chicken Parmesan and pizza and will often add it to green beans or cauliflower. I even use it to make Tomato Soup (page 44).

Got Carb Counters? / People these days are so against eating carbs, but I'm a huge believer in portion control. I never deprive myself of pasta if I want it—I'm Italian, after all. That said, I don't eat a huge bowl, and if there are nights I do indulge, I just plan on working out a little harder the next day. Once, when my father was visiting, I put out a bowl of pasta in the center of the table. When he sat down he pulled it towards his seat and said, "This is for me, right, babe? What are you feeding the boys?" I was like, "Dad, that bowl's for everybody!"

TORTA DELLA NONNA

I learned this recipe in a cooking class I took in Florence. I love Florence. I'd rent an apartment there for a month at a time, if only I could speak Italian. Maybe one day I'll hire some fine, young, (obviously gorgeous) Italian man to be my escort/interpreter...

Serves: 8

PIE PASTRY

- 2 cups flour
- Pinch iodized salt
- ⅔ cup sugar
- Zest of 2 lemons (use Microplane)
- 1 cup unsalted butter, room temperature
- 4 egg yolks

CUSTARD

- 2 cups milk
- 2 oranges, juice and zest
- 3 egg yolks
- Pinch iodized salt
- ½ cup of sugar
- 4 tablespoons flour

DECORATIONS

- Slivered almonds (optional)
- Confectioners' sugar

1 You'll need a 10" spring form pan. Preheat oven to 400 degrees.

2 FOR THE PIE PASTRY: Mix flour with salt, sugar, and lemon zest. Add butter in pieces and mix with fingers until crumbly. Add the yolks and mix.

3 On top of parchment paper, roll out the pastry in two circles making one slightly bigger. Place smaller ring into the bottom of a 10" spring form pan, bringing up the sides just slightly. Save the larger dough circle for the top. Wrap in parchment paper and place in refrigerator while making custard.

4 FOR THE CUSTARD: Bring the milk, grated orange zest, and juice to a boil.

5 In a metal bowl, whisk the yolks with salt and sugar until white and fluffy. Add the flour to yolks and stir. Gradually add boiled milk to the metal bowl and stir to combine.

6 Put custard back into pot on stove. Bring to a boil and cook for 3 minutes, stirring constantly. (Okay, I agree this is time consuming but trust me, it's delicious!)

7 Pour custard back into the metal bowl, then place that bowl into a larger bowl filled with ice and water. Cool the custard for approximately 10 to 15 minutes. Once cooled, place custard on top of pie pastry in the spring form pan, then carefully add the top layer of pie pastry. Sprinkle top with slivered almonds (optional).

8 Bake for 30 minutes. Cool completely and remove outer sides of spring form pan. Sprinkle with confectioners' sugar and serve.

BOOK CLUB DINNER

» I have been lucky enough to be in a book club now for over 15 years. We have shared life experiences as well as books. We started ours when our children were in grade school and now it's lovely to see photos from their weddings and even experience the births of their babies. The trick to cooking for a book club is to have everything made in advance and serve it all at once, because you don't want to miss out on the conversations. This menu has a bowl of stew and the salad is served on the side along with bread. I've paired it with cookies, which can be passed easily around the table, and I offer pears for those who don't want the added calories of baked goods.

MENU

Short Rib Stew in Red Wine Sauce

Fresh Bread

Kale Salad with Dried Cranberries and Toasted Pecans in Honey Dijon Vinaigrette

WINE / 2010 Sandrone Barolo 'Le Vigne' (Piedmont, Italy)

Assorted Cheeses Sprinkled with Poppy Seeds and Drizzled with Honey

WINE / 2010 Baumard Quarts de Chaume (Loire Valley, France)

Pears and Nutella for dipping

Molasses Cookies

ENTERTAINING NOTES

3 DAYS BEFORE / Set table. Prepare playlist. Choose and purchase wine.

2 DAYS BEFORE / Food shop (including meat).

1 DAY BEFORE / Make stew.

DAY OF DINNER / Remove stew from refrigerator. Skim fat. Clean kale and make Honey Dijon Vinaigrette. Put kale and dressing back in refrigerator. Toast pecans and leave out to cool.

JUST BEFORE GUESTS ARRIVE / Reheat stew.

Prepare cheese plate. Take out fruit and place in a nice bowl. Take out Nutella. Place cookies on a nice tray.

WHEN GUESTS ARRIVE / Toss salad. Serve stew and salad together. Put out a basket of bread to pass.

AFTER CLEARING PLATES / Drizzle honey over cut pieces of cheese and sprinkle with poppy seeds. Serve at center of table with individual plates so people can help themselves. Put out pears and Nutella. Put out cookies to be passed.

PLAYLIST

15 Step Radiohead / **I Feel Like Funkin' It Up** Rebirth Brass Band / **The House That Jack Built** Aretha Franklin / **Never Give You Up** Raphael Saadiq / **Forever Mine** Andra Day / **Retrograde** James Blake / **As** Stevie Wonder / **Autumn Leaves** Eva Cassidy / **Can I Get a Witness** Marvin Gaye / **Bottom of the River** Delta Rae / **Something to Talk About** Bonnie Raitt / **I Learned the Hard Way** Sharon Jones / **Fool for You** Alice Smith / **Sexual Healing** The Hot 8 Brass Band / **Dorothy Dandridge Eyes** Esperanza Spaulding and Janelle Monae / **Cream** Prince

1 HOUR, 5 MINUTES; PLAYLIST AND SONGS AVAILABLE ON SPOTIFY (MEGANOBLOCK)

SHORT RIB STEW IN A RED WINE SAUCE

I made this for a book group dinner and learned a valuable lesson. The table was set with a fork to the left and a knife to the right. After cooking for two hours, the meat comes out like butter (or as we pronounce it in New Jersey, "butta"). No knife needed—unless, of course, you're serving butter with your bread (and you must have bread for sopping up the gravy). But the ladies asked for a spoon so they could get all that gorgeous gravy, which I took as a huge compliment. Bottom line: Serve this dish with a big soup spoon!

Serves: 12

4 pounds boneless beef short ribs, cut into 1 inch pieces

½ cup flour (adding more if needed to coat all pieces of meat)

3 tablespoons olive oil (adding more if needed with each batch)

3 cups red wine (oh, hell, pour the whole bottle in)

3 cups broth (veal stock is preferable, if you can find it. Otherwise, use beef or chicken)

6-8 carrots, sliced (if very large, cut in half before slicing)

3-4 Yukon gold potatoes, peeled and cut into ½ inch pieces

3-4 parsnips, peeled and cut into ½ inch pieces

½-1 onions, cut into 1 inch pieces (I don't like a lot of onions)

½-1 pound cremini mushrooms, quartered (I love mushrooms)

1 tablespoon fresh thyme, chopped (a hassle, I know, but so great)

8 fresh sage leaves, chopped

Kosher salt and freshly ground pepper

1 In a Ziploc bag, toss the short ribs with the flour. Heat oil in a large pot and sauté your ribs a few at a time over medium heat until browned all over, about 6 minutes per batch.

2 Return all the meat and all the juices back into the pot. Add the wine and increase heat for about 5 minutes. Add the stock, lower the heat, and cover until meat is tender, about 2 hours.

3 Stir in the carrots, potatoes, parsnips, onion, mushrooms, thyme, and sage. Cover and simmer over low heat until the vegetables are tender, about 30 minutes. Season with salt and pepper to taste.

4 Make a day in advance and refrigerate. The next day, skim off the fat and reheat covered in 350 degree oven for approximately 45 minutes. If it needs more gravy, add a cup of beef or veal broth while reheating.

5 Serve with crusty bread or rolls.

KALE SALAD WITH DRIED CRANBERRIES AND TOASTED PECANS IN HONEY DIJON VINAIGRETTE

Everyone knows that kale is good for you. Growing up, we only had it on Thanksgiving, when my mother boiled the hell out of it and depleted all its nutrients. We don't do that anymore. For this salad, apply your vinaigrette five to ten minutes before serving so that the kale gets tender.

Serves: 8

- ¾ cup chopped pecans
- 1 tablespoon Dijon mustard
- 1 tablespoon honey
- 2 tablespoons cider vinegar
- 3 tablespoons olive oil
  Kosher salt and freshly ground pepper
- 1 teaspoon fresh thyme, chopped
- 5 ounces kale*
- ¾ cup dried cranberries
- ½ cup Parmesan cheese, grated

1 In a skillet over medium to high heat, toast pecans, stirring often for about three minutes. Set aside to cool.

2 For the Vinaigrette: In a bowl, whisk together mustard, honey, and vinegar and salt and pepper to taste. Slowly drizzle in olive oil, whisking constantly. Stir in thyme.

3 In a large bowl, combine kale with pecans and dried cranberries. Toss the vinaigrette and sprinkle cheese on top.

A NOTE ON KALE

*There are so many varieties of kale available now. If you can find baby kale, you do not have to chop it. Larger, rougher kales should have their stems cut away and the leaves sliced thinly.

Pears and Nutella
for dipping

Assorted Cheeses
Sprinkled with Poppy
Seeds and Drizzled
with Honey (right)

MOLASSES COOKIES

I love the smell of my kitchen when I am baking these cookies, a classic molasses cookie with a soft, chewy center. Once the fall comes, I'm driven to baking them.

Makes: 2½ dozen

2   cups flour

2   teaspoons baking soda

1   teaspoon each ginger,* ground cloves, and cinnamon

¾   cup (1½ sticks) sweet unsalted butter

1   cup granulated sugar, plus extra for rolling

¼   cup molasses

1 egg, beaten

1 Preheat oven to 350 degrees.

2 Lightly grease baking sheets with butter or line them with parchment paper.

3 In a medium bowl, combine flour, baking soda, and spices. You can sift, though I don't always.

4 In a larger bowl, beat butter and sugar. Add molasses and beaten egg. Add the dry ingredients to the butter mixture and combine. Roll into small balls, about a large tablespoon-full at a time.

5 OPTIONAL STEP: Pour sugar into a pie plate, and roll the balls in the sugar. As the years go by, I have started to exclude this step—less sugar in our diets is better, and they are still delicious.

6 Place cookies on the prepared baking sheets, leaving 2 inches between each cookie. Bake 8 to 10 minutes.

A NOTE ON GINGER

*If you really like the taste of ginger, add a little more. As always, experiment! Make these the way your family likes them. Some kids like more cinnamon and less ginger.

WINTER

HEART TO TABLE

MENU

Nuts, Cheeses, Crackers,
Grapes, and Fig Jam

Crudité with Tuscan
White Bean Dip

Shots of Tomato Soup

Tuscan-Style Pulled
Pork Sandwiches

Coleslaw with
Buttermilk Dressing

Platter of Prosciutto,
Mozzarella, Tomatoes,
and Lettuce

Roasted Red Peppers, Pesto,
Aged Balsamic Vinegar

Focaccia and Italian Rolls

Penne with Pesto

Green Salad with
Red Wine Vinaigrette
and Italian Herbs*

Citrus Salad
with Mint Sugar

Ricotta Cookies

WINE

RED / 2014 Tenuta
Sant'Antonio Scaia Corvino
(Veneto, Italy)

WHITE / 2014 Villa Matilde
Greco di Tufo
(Campania, Italy)

» Everybody enjoys being invited to watch a Super Bowl game with friends. Come to think of it, any football game is more fun when shared with a group. This menu is my Italian twist on a classic, all-American Super Bowl party (with the bonus addition of healthy choices for those who don't eat pasta or bread). Many of these recipes can be made in advance, and eaten throughout the next week. The Pesto can be used as a spread on sandwiches and added to pasta, while the White Bean Dip makes a great crudité that's just as good the next day as soup. You can also have fun using sugar in your favorite team's colors on top of the Ricotta Cookies. And, of course, some items can be bought, like bowls of nuts, platters of cheese, crackers, and grapes. Put out platters of prosciutto, tomatoes, mozzarella and lettuce with focaccia and Italian rolls. Not everything has to be made from scratch.

SUPER BOWL PARTY

ENTERTAINING NOTES

3 DAYS BEFORE / Set table. Prepare playlist. Choose and purchase wine and beer. Place stick'ems on bowls and platters you will be using. Soak white beans overnight.

2 DAYS BEFORE / Food shop (including meat but not rolls). Make Tomato Soup. Make Tuscan White Bean Dip. Make Pesto. Apply dry rub to pork. Make Ricotta Cookies. Make vinaigrette for salad.

1 DAY BEFORE / Buy rolls for pulled pork sandwiches. Buy flowers. Make pork and coleslaw. Cut up citrus for salad and put in refrigerator. Make mint and sugar mixture (but leave out on counter). Make Roasted Red Peppers. Clean and cut vegetables for crudité. Clean grapes and cut into bunches (I like to do this for guests so that they can grab a bunch at a time).

DAY OF PARTY / Put cookies on a nice tray. Clean lettuce for salad, and cut cucumbers and tomatoes and put back in refrigerator. Make penne (or whatever pasta you are using with the Pesto), rinse in very cold water, strain (but save water) and place pasta in refrigerator in Ziploc bag. Two hours before guests arrive, remove soup, pork, Roasted Red Peppers, Pesto, and Tuscan White Bean Dip from refrigerator.

JUST BEFORE GUESTS ARRIVE / Put out nuts, platter of cheese and grapes, crudité, platter of prosciutto and mozzarella, and Roasted Red Peppers. Put soup on low. Preheat oven to 350 degrees. Put pork in oven for 30 minutes. Sauté penne in Pesto on very low heat, adding strained water to achieve the consistency you like and cover pan cooking on low until heated through. Toss salad with vinaigrette just before putting out, as you don't want lettuce to get "wimpy."

WHEN GUESTS ARRIVE / Serve tomato soup while pork is warming in the oven. Remove rolls from packaging five minutes before serving sandwiches; cover tightly with tin foil and warm in oven for 5 minutes.

A NOTE ON SALADS

*It is always good to have a simple tossed green salad on a buffet table. For suggestions on salads, see pages 18, 32, and 60.

PLAYLIST

Sound and Color Alabama Shakes / **The Suburbs** Arcade Fire / **Tennessee Whiskey** Chris Stapleton / **Betray My Heart** D'Angelo and the Vanguard / **Marfa Lights** Steelism / **Under the Pressure** War on Drugs / **Right Time** Nikki Lane / **Between the Devil and the Deep Blue Sea** The Arcs / **Hope of a Lifetime** Milk Carton Kids / **Mykonos** Fleet Foxes / **Blue Lady** Rene Aubry / **City of New Orleans** Willie Nelson / **Natural Mystic** Bob Marley / **Furr** Blitzen Trapper / **Meet Me in the City** Junior Kimbrough / **Little Walter Rides Again** Medeski, Scofield, Martin & Wood / **I Don't Feel Like Dancin'** The Scissor Sisters / **Give Me the Night** George Benson / **Atlantic City** The Band / **Sweet Virginia** Rolling Stones / **The Less I Know the Better** Tame Impala / **New Slang** The Shins / **Why Is It So Hard** Charles Bradley / **Mama Why You Don't Like My Man** Sharon Jones and the Dap Kings / **Lady on the Water** Blitzen Trapper / **Go Home** Lucius / **Please Read the Letter** Robert Plant and Alison Krauss / **You Know I'm No Good** Amy Winehouse

2 HOURS; PLAYLIST AND SONGS AVAILABLE ON SPOTIFY (MEGANOBLOCK)

TUSCAN WHITE BEAN DIP (OR SOUP)

This is a very versatile recipe that can be used as a dip for crudité, added to toasted Italian bread for bruschetta with Slow-Roasted Tomatoes (page 58) on top, and as a thick creamy bean soup. I make a large batch of it and use it in all different ways throughout the week.

Serves: 6 to 8

---

1 16-ounce bag white beans, soaked overnight in cold water

1 yellow onion, diced (about 1 cup)*

4 garlic cloves, peeled and chopped

¼ cup fresh Italian flat leaf parsley, chopped

3 sprigs fresh rosemary, chopped (could substitute sage, if preferred)

2 celery stalks, chopped

4 tablespoons olive oil

6 cups water or vegetable broth

2 hambones (or 8 slices of prosciutto)**

Kosher salt and freshly ground pepper

Parmesan cheese, grated

1 Combine onion, garlic, parsley, rosemary, and celery in a large pot, and sauté in the olive oil at medium heat for approximately 5 to 8 minutes to create a soffritto. Add drained beans and sauté for approximately 3 to 5 minutes, stirring often.

2 Fill the pot with water or broth to cover the beans (approximately 6 cups).

3 Add hambones or prosciutto (if using) and gently cook, uncovered, for 2 hours, stirring occasionally and adding fresh water if needed until beans are soft and consistency is creamy. Remove hambones. If using prosciutto, leave in.

4 Using a ladle take soup in batches and add to Cuisinart or blender, then return back to pot. This creates a thick, creamy bean dip or soup.

5 Add salt and pepper to taste. This can and should be made one day in advance, as all soups taste better the next day.

6 Serve with a drizzle of olive oil and grated Parmesan cheese to taste.

ADDITIONAL NOTES

*Be careful! Onions and white beans are very personal. In some households, the combination could be grounds for divorce. If this is true for you, try substituting leeks or shallots for the onions.

**Could leave out meat and make this completely vegetarian.

TOMATO SOUP

I make this soup all year 'round. It's a modified version of my Fuggedaboutit Tomato Gravy (page 20). Orange zest added just before serving lightens up the flavor beautifully.

Serves: 8

¼ cup olive oil

3 garlic cloves, crushed

1 28-ounce can
   San Marzano whole peeled
   plum tomatoes, blended

1 6-ounce can tomato paste

¾ cup vegetable broth

1 teaspoon dried herbs
   (dill, basil, or oregano)

   Kosher salt and
   freshly ground pepper

   Zest of 1 orange
   (use Microplane)

1 In large pot, sauté olive oil and garlic on medium heat for 1 to 2 minutes, being careful not to burn. Add tomatoes and continue to cook for 10 more minutes.

2 Add paste, vegetable broth, and herbs (if you opt to use fresh herbs, double the amount). Stir to combine and continue to simmer on medium heat for another 10 minutes. Check for consistency. If the soup is too thick, add more vegetable broth. Add salt and pepper to taste.

3 Just before serving, top each cup with orange zest.

TUSCAN-STYLE PULLED PORK SANDWICHES

I learned this recipe while on a cooking vacation in Florence. We had the amazing opportunity to be in a fantastic kitchen in a villa in the hills of Tuscany observing a fantastic Italian woman. When you make this dish, the kitchen smells gorgeous—the combination of rosemary, balsamic vinegar, and white wine...mmm. I made a mistake and bought the wrong cut of pork, but realized it was a "happy mistake" and decided to make pulled pork sandwiches with it.

This recipe calls for a lot of fresh thyme. Thyme can be a bitch to work with—you have to slide all those little leaves off the branch. I remember a sweet 7th grade boy in my inner city volunteer cooking class who hated working with thyme. He used to get a girl in the class to do it for him. I loved how he cleverly delegated the job he disliked doing. I'll bet he's a big wig executive now—at least I hope so.

Serves: 10

4-5 pounds boneless pork shoulder or Boston Butt

2 teaspoons Kosher salt

2 tablespoons freshly ground pepper (approximately 30 turns of the pepper mill)

6 tablespoons fresh thyme, chopped

6 tablespoons fresh rosemary, chopped

4 garlic cloves, chopped

6 tablespoons olive oil

⅔ cup balsamic vinegar

2 cups white wine

1½ ounces veal Demi-Glace Gold, Classic French Demi-Glace (available on Amazon.com or use 3 tablespoons tomato paste)

1 Combine salt, pepper, thyme, rosemary, and garlic in a large bowl. Place pork shoulder in bowl and rub with herb mixture to cover. Remove pork from bowl and wrap in plastic and refrigerate overnight, or for at least 6 hours.

2 Preheat oven to 325 degrees. Gently heat olive oil in a large pot. Add pork and brown, approximately 2 minutes on each side. Add vinegar and white wine. Cover pot and place in oven. Cook for 3 to 4 hours, turning once every hour. (Careful not to burn your fingers like I did! Such a dumbass...)

3 When cooked, remove meat, place on a cutting board, and cover with foil. Set aside.

4 To the pan of juices, add demi-glace or tomato paste to thicken. Turn up heat slightly to evaporate some of the alcohol, while scraping bits from bottom of pot. Cook for approximately 5 minutes. Turn off heat.

5 Remove netting (which is how the pork shoulder comes from the butcher) and use two forks to shred meat, removing the fatty parts. Return shredded pork to pot of juices to let it soak up all that yumminess!

6 Can be made one day in advance. To serve, remove from refrigerator one hour before reheating. Skim off fat. Reheat in 325 degree oven, covered, for approximately 30 to 45 minutes.

ROASTED RED PEPPERS

« You will often see these at an Italian restaurant as an antipasti option. I serve them by themselves, in sub sandwiches, or over pesto on bruschetta. Warning: This is a fair amount of work, but they are so superior to store-bought peppers.

Serves: 8

6 red bell peppers

2 garlic cloves, thinly sliced

1 teaspoon olive oil

1 teaspoon balsamic vinegar

1 tablespoon fresh oregano or basil (or ½ tablespoon dried)

Kosher salt and freshly ground pepper

1 Preheat oven to broil or put grill on highest level. Place cleaned whole peppers on a baking sheet in broiler or directly on grill. Turn peppers to blacken on all sides, approximately 10 to 15 minutes total.

2 Place peppers in a large bowl and cover with foil for 10 minutes. Peel peppers and cut into strips removing seeds and saving as much juice as possible.

3 Sprinkle on top of peppers the garlic, olive oil, vinegar, oregano (or basil), and salt and pepper to taste.

COLESLAW WITH BUTTERMILK DRESSING

There are so many ways of making coleslaw. I tried several and this recipe was the winner. It's great on pulled pork sandwiches, but also on its own. I've also substituted cilantro for the parsley and lime for the lemon—a version that works especially well with chicken breasts. You can also use the dressing on green salads.

Serves: 10 to 12

1 head cabbage, cored and shredded (about 12 cups)

1 cup buttermilk

⅔ cup mayonnaise

1 cup fresh Italian flat leaf parsley, chopped finely

2 garlic cloves, minced (use Microplane)

Juice of 1 lemon

Kosher salt and freshly ground pepper

1 Whisk together all ingredients but cabbage in a large bowl.

2 Add shredded cabbage and mix thoroughly. Taste and correct for seasoning, adding more salt and pepper if necessary. Refrigerate before serving.

PESTO

You can do so much with this pesto besides serve it with pasta. Maybe you want to add pesto to a plate of tomatoes and mozzarella. You can also spread some on toasted slices of Italian bread and top with Slow-Roasted Tomatoes (page 58) for a wonderful bruschetta. In the summer months, I serve this Pesto on individual plates beneath sliced peaches and tomatoes for a beautiful first course.

Makes: 1 pint

---

6 garlic cloves
(less if you prefer)

1 cup pine nuts

8 cups fresh basil
(1 ounce of loose basil
= 2 cups)

Juice of 1 lemon

Kosher salt and
freshly ground pepper

Parmesan cheese,
grated

¼ cup olive oil
(more if necessary to
ensure proper consistency)

Heavy or light cream
(optional)

1 Using Cuisinart, pulse garlic and pine nuts until a dough forms. Add basil and continue to pulse, using a spatula to clean the sides of the bowl. Add lemon juice and a pinch of salt, pepper, and some grated Parmesan cheese (one tablespoon for starters). You can always add more later, but you can't take it back.

2 Pulse again until blended. While machine is still running add olive oil to the top streamer. Taste and correct for seasoning and consistency. If it's too thick, add more olive oil.

3 And that's it! Use with any type of hot, strained pasta. To adjust the consistency of your pasta, save some of the strained water and add back to pasta and pesto mix a bit at a time.

OPTIONAL: If you like your pesto creamier, add some light or heavy cream.

CITRUS SALAD WITH MINT SUGAR

I always like having a healthy choice for guests. Sure, there is some sugar in this, but not a lot—and it's a lovely palate cleanser. This salad can be made one day ahead.

Serves: 6

- 2 white grapefruits
- 2 pink grapefruits
- 6 large navel oranges
- ½ cup fresh mint leaves (if dried, use less)
- 2 tablespoons sugar (or less if you prefer)

1 Peel the skin and flesh from your fruit. I find a serrated knife works best for this. Cut up segments and place in a bowl. Careful not to get any white parts in your salad and obviously no pits. (That is obvious, right? Don't you make me come over to your kitchen and slap you upside the head like they do in some Italian-American households!) Be sure to grab all the juices into the bowl. Refrigerate.

2 Place mint and sugar in food processor or very finely chop mint by hand and combine with sugar. Keep out on counter.

3 When ready to serve, sprinkle mint and sugar mixture over fruit.

RICOTTA COOKIES

My best friend, Lydia, was from what I would call a "really Italian" family. I would go to her house on a Sunday and there would be massive amounts of aunts, uncles, and cousins eating massive amounts of food. At the end of their meal, which lasted the entire day, they would serve these cookies. If you're making for a Super Bowl party, you can color the glaze to coordinate with the team colors, or you can keep the glaze white and use colored sugar or sprinkles on top to coordinate with team colors.

Makes: 8 dozen

COOKIES

- 2 cups flour
- ½ teaspoon baking soda
- ½ teaspoon baking powder
- ½ cup unsalted butter (1 stick), at room temperature
- 1 cup sugar
- 1 egg
- 1 cup whole-milk ricotta cheese
- 1 teaspoon vanilla extract

GLAZE

- ¾ cup confectioners' sugar
- 4 teaspoons whole milk
- Lemon juice, just a little squeeze
- Colored sprinkles, for garnish

1 Preheat oven to 350 degrees.

2 Lightly grease baking sheets with butter or line them with parchment paper. Measure then sift together the flour, baking soda, and baking powder in a medium bowl. Set aside.

3 In a large bowl with electric mixer, beat the butter and sugar at low speed until smooth. Add egg and continue beating. Add the ricotta and vanilla and beat just until the mixture is smooth. With the mixer set on low speed, add the flour mixture to the batter and blend.

4 Roll the batter into tablespoon-sized mounds (like little meatballs) and place on the prepared baking sheets, leaving 1 inch between each cookie. (Size is important. Sometimes I make them too big.) Bake for 12 minutes. You want these cookies to be quite white and soft.

5 Transfer to a wire rack to cool, but keep in mind that if you are going to add the glaze, the cookies need to be on the warm side, so make the glaze immediately.

6 FOR THE GLAZE: In a small bowl, use a whisk to stir the confectioners' sugar, slowly adding milk, 1 teaspoon at a time, continuing to stir until the mixture is a pourable consistency. Whisk in the lemon juice. Add more milk if necessary to create a consistency that's liquid enough to drizzle onto the cookies.

7 Glaze the still-warm cookies and add the colored sprinkles, if using. I don't glaze and sprinkle all of the cookies. I like to leave some without the extra sugar on top. Store in an airtight container layered with wax paper. Can keep in the freezer for up to two weeks.

» I enjoy gathering single friends over for a Valentine's-themed dinner party. This menu is purposefully loaded with aphrodisiacs. When you say "aphrodisiac," everyone immediately thinks oysters but many food items can be classified as such, based on their shape, texture, and ability to increase blood flow. Throw a party like this and see what happens—either your single friends will connect or the eyes of your married couples might wander!

VALENTINE'S DAY DINNER

APHRODISIACS

Bruschetta with
Pesto and Slow-Roasted
Tomatoes

Arugula Salad
with Avocado
and Tomatoes in
Balsamic Vinaigrette

WINE / 2014 Hopler
Gruner Veltliner
(Burgenland, Austria)

Baked Salmon
with Ginger Sauce

Broccoli with
Honey Vinaigrette

Caramelized Coriander
Roasted Carrots

WINE / 2013 Domaine
Weinbach Gewurztraminer
'Reserve Personelle'
(Alsace, France)

Chocolate Molten
Lava Cake
with Fresh
Whipped Cream

WINE / 2013 Chapoutier
Banyuls
(Roussillon, France)

ENTERTAINING NOTES

3 DAYS BEFORE / Set table. Prepare playlist. Choose and purchase wines.

2 DAYS BEFORE / Food shop (except fish). Make Pesto and Slow-Roasted Tomatoes.

1 DAY BEFORE / Make Ginger Sauce, Chocolate Molten Lava Cakes (and freeze), and Honey Vinaigrette.

DAY OF DINNER / Buy fish, clean, pat dry, and refrigerate. Clean lettuce, peel and cut carrots, clean and cut broccoli, and put in refrigerator. Clean and cut tomatoes for salad and put in refrigerator. Mid-day, remove Ginger Sauce, Honey Vinaigrette, Pesto, and Slow-Roasted Tomatoes from refrigerator. Whip cream and refrigerate.

JUST BEFORE GUESTS ARRIVE / Remove salmon

from refrigerator, place in a baking dish, pour on ginger sauce, and cover tightly with foil. Preheat oven. Prepare carrots and broccoli. Start Bruschetta.

WHEN GUESTS ARRIVE / Cut up avocado, add tomatoes, and toss salad with olive oil and vinegar. Place on table. Spread Pesto on toasted bread and cover with tomatoes, and bake. Place salmon in oven along with carrots and broccoli. Just before salmon is done, toss broccoli in Honey Vinaigrette. After salmon is done, increase oven temperature to 400 degrees for the Lava Cakes later.

AFTER EATING DINNER / Remove Lava Cakes from freezer and bake. Remove whipped cream from refrigerator.

PLAYLIST

Let's Stay Together Al Green / **Sex Bomb** Tom Jones / **Radar Love** Golden Earring / **All You Need Is Love** Beatles / **Mirrors** Justin Timberlake / **Love Shack** The B-52's / **Game of Love** Daft Punk / **All My Love** Led Zeppelin / **Untitled (How Does It Feel)** D'Angelo / **Brown Sugar** D'Angelo / **Really Love** D'Angelo and The Vanguard / **Sex Machine** James Brown / **The Way You Make Me Feel** Michael Jackson / **Is This Love** Bob Marley / **I Want to Be Your Man** Zap and Roger / **You Send Me** Sam Cooke / **The Power of Love** Huey Lewis and the News / **My Girl** Rolling Stones / **Love Me Tender** Elvis Presley / **This Will Be (An Everlasting Love)** Natalie Cole / **I Will** Beatles / **Can't Take My Eyes Off of You** Lauryn Hill

1 HOUR, 37 MINUTES; PLAYLIST AND SONGS AVAILABLE ON SPOTIFY (MEGANOBLOCK)

SLOW-ROASTED TOMATOES

This recipe is ridiculously easy. These tomatoes can be made in advance, refrigerated, and then reheated. I serve them with fish, chicken, pasta, and cold rice salads, and often add to green salads. For Valentine's Day, I like using them to make bruschetta. Just toast sliced Italian bread, brush olive oil on each slice, and spread with Pesto (page 50) or Tuscan White Bean Dip (page 42), and place these tomatoes on top. Bake for 3 minutes in 350 degree oven. Delish!

Serves: 10

2   pints of cherry tomatoes, halved

2   tablespoons olive oil

1   teaspoon sugar (optional)

1   teaspoon red wine vinegar or balsamic vinegar

Handful of fresh thyme leaves or fresh marjoram leaves

Kosher salt and fresh ground pepper

1 You'll need a 9″ x 13″ baking dish. Preheat oven to 250 degrees.

2 Line a baking dish with parchment paper or tin foil.

3 Toss tomatoes in baking dish with olive oil, sugar (if using), vinegar, and herbs and salt and pepper to taste. Roast for one hour until tomatoes are soft, stirring halfway through baking time.

4 Let cool and refrigerate if not using immediately.

ARUGULA SALAD WITH AVOCADO AND TOMATOES IN BALSAMIC VINAIGRETTE

There is really no recipe here per se because it's just a wonderful salad loaded with aphrodisiacs. Arugula has been documented as an aphrodisiac since the first century A.D. probably because of its peppery taste. The Aztecs called the avocado tree "Ahuacuati," which translated means "testicle tree." When buying avocadoes, be sure they are on the softer side. Add tomatoes, toss this salad with a high quality extra virgin olive oil and balsamic vinegar, and add a pinch of kosher salt and freshly ground pepper.

SALMON WITH GINGER SAUCE

Guests love this dish. I learned to make it while taking a cooking class in Paris from Chef Samira, a chef with Internationalkitchen.com. What works so well for entertaining is that you can make the ginger sauce the day before.

Serves: 6

---

8 tablespoons olive oil, divided

4 shallots, minced

1 cup white wine

8 tablespoons brown sugar (light or dark)

½ cup low sodium soy sauce

Juice of 2 lemons

3 garlic cloves, minced

8-12 tablespoons ginger root, minced (about 6 to 8 inches of ginger root)

½ teaspoon of cayenne pepper (optional)

6 salmon fillets, 5 to 6 ounces each

1 You'll need a 9″ x 13″ baking dish. Preheat oven to 350 degrees.

2 Heat 4 tablespoons of olive oil in a medium pan. Add shallots and sauté on medium heat for 4 minutes. Stir occasionally, being careful not to burn. Add wine and cook another 3 minutes.

3 Add remaining ingredients except salmon and cook for 5 minutes. Remove from heat and set aside.

4 Place salmon in baking dish. Pour ginger sauce on top of salmon and cover tightly with tin foil.

5 Bake for approximately 30 minutes. You could also opt to grill the salmon, and add the sauce afterwards.

BROCCOLI WITH HONEY VINAIGRETTE

I also learned this recipe in a cooking class in Paris. I drizzle it on top of any vegetable. In this menu, I put it on broccoli or broccoli rabe, if available. It keeps in the refrigerator for up to 1 week.

Serves: 6

3 heads broccoli, cut into florets (approximately 4 cups)

2 tablespoons olive oil

1 green onion (green part only), cut into 2-inch pieces

2 tablespoons Italian flat leaf parsley, chopped

2 tablespoons low sodium soy sauce

2 tablespoons raw honey (the thick, nearly solid kind)

2 tablespoons white wine vinegar

1 cup olive oil

1 FOR THE BROCCOLI: You'll need a 9" x 13" baking dish or a cast iron pan. Preheat oven to 400 degrees.

2 Toss broccoli in baking dish with olive oil. Roast for 20 minutes, stirring halfway through. When ready to serve, toss broccoli with the honey vinaigrette.

3 FOR THE HONEY VINAIGRETTE: Toss all ingredients in a blender and blend until creamy.

CARAMELIZED CORIANDER ROASTED CARROTS

I make these carrots often. They are easy and healthy.

Serves: 6

12 medium to large carrots, peeled, cut on diagonal into 1-inch pieces (approximately 2 cups)

2 tablespoons olive oil

1½ teaspoons ground coriander or cumin

Kosher salt and freshly ground pepper

1 You'll need a 9″ x 13″ baking dish or a cast iron pan. Preheat oven to 400 degrees.

2 Toss carrots in baking dish with olive oil and herbs, and salt and pepper to taste. Roast until tender and lightly caramelized, approximately 35 minutes, stirring halfway through.

CHOCOLATE MOLTEN LAVA CAKE WITH FRESH WHIPPED CREAM

This is an easy recipe that can be made in advance. Guests will be dazzled!

Serves: 4

CAKE

- 7 ounces dark chocolate (60% cocoa is nice)
- 4 tablespoons unsalted butter
- ½ cup confectioners' sugar
- 4 eggs
- Pinch of iodized salt
- 2 tablespoons flour, sifted
- 4 ramekins or aluminum cups

WHIPPED CREAM

- 2 cups (1 pint) heavy cream
- 2 tablespoons confectioners' sugar
- Nutmeg (optional)

1 Grease and flour ramekins or metal cups. You can also use a butter spray.

2 Melt chocolate with butter and sugar on very low heat in a medium pot. Add the eggs one at a time, whisking to combine each time. Add pinch of salt and flour. Use a whisk to mix.

3 Pour mixture into prepared ramekins. Cover with plastic and put in freezer for minimum of 1 hour, up to 24 hours.

4 Remove from freezer and place on cookie sheet. Remove plastic. Cook frozen at 400 degrees for 10 minutes. Slide knife around edge and flip over onto plate. Serve immediately with whipped cream.

5 FOR THE WHIPPED CREAM: With an electric mixer on high blend until thick. Could add freshly grated nutmeg on top.

APHRODISIACS

ARUGULA / Arugula has been documented as an aphrodisiac since the first century A.D., when it was added to grated orchid bulbs and parsnips, and combined with pine nuts and pistachios.

AVOCADO / The Aztecs called the avocado tree "Ahuacuati," or "testicle tree." The ancients thought the fruit hanging in pairs on the tree resembled the male's testicles. This fruit also has a sensuous texture.

BASIL / Said to stimulate the sex drive and boost fertility, as well as to produce a general sense of well-being for body and mind.

BROCCOLI / The ground seeds of various plants in the brassica family were believed to increase virility. In the case of broccoli rabe, it's more likely a myth created to get people to eat the bitter green vegetable.

CHOCOLATE / Chocolate, which the Aztecs referred to as "nourishment of the Gods," contains chemicals thought to affect neurotransmitters in the brain and a related substance to caffeine called theobromine. Chocolate contains more antioxidants than red wine. The secret for passion is to combine the two.

CARROTS / The phallus-shaped carrot has been associated with stimulation since ancient times and was used by early Middle Eastern royalty to aid seduction.

CORIANDER / *The Arabian Nights* tells a tale of a merchant who had been childless for 40 years but was cured by a concoction that included coriander.

GARLIC / The "heat" in garlic is said to stir sexual desires. Make sure you and your partner share it together. Garlic has been used for centuries to cure everything from the common cold to heart ailments. This is a good time for moderation.

GINGER / Raw, cooked, or crystallized, ginger is a stimulant to the circulatory system.

HONEY / Many medicines in Egyptian times were based on honey, including cures for sterility and impotence. Medieval seducers plied their partners with mead, a fermented honey drink. Lovers on their "Honeymoon" drank mead and it was thought to "sweeten" the marriage.

NUTMEG / Nutmeg was highly prized by Chinese women as an aphrodisiac. In quantity, nutmeg can be hallucinogenic.

OLIVE OIL / Packed with antioxidants, olives and their oil have been used for centuries for health. The Greeks believed they made men more virile as well.

PINE NUTS / Zinc is a key mineral necessary to maintain male potency and pine nuts are rich in zinc. Pine nuts have been used to stimulate the libido as far back as medieval times.

SALMON / Salmon often gets the nod as one of the healthiest fish you can eat—not only a great source of protein to help build lean muscle, which alone would improve your sex life, but also rich in omega-3s, which can lead to increased levels of serotonin that, in turn, leads to an improved mood and mental state, making you more likely to initiate sex and enjoy it as well. The pink, velvety texture of a salmon fillet is also stimulating to the senses.

VANILLA / The scent and flavor of vanilla is believed to increase lust. According to the Australian Orchid Society, "Old Totonac lore has it that Xanat, the young daughter of the Mexican fertility goddess, loved a Totonac youth. Unable to marry him due to her divine nature, she transformed herself into a plant that would provide pleasure and happiness." That plant was the vanilla orchid.

WINE / A glass or two of wine can greatly enhance a romantic interlude. Wine relaxes and helps to stimulate the senses, while the act of drinking wine can be an erotic experience. Let your eyes feast on the color of the liquid. Caress the glass, savor the taste on your lips. Do remember, however, that excessive alcohol will make you too drowsy for the after-dinner romance.

SPRING

HEART TO TABLE

EASTER LUNCH

» Gathering with family for holidays is so special. With my three sons living in different cities now, I find it especially important. This Easter menu has a Rack, of Lamb, which was always a favorite for my boys. I put this recipe in my first cookbook, *Cooking for My 3 Sons*, as well because it's such a great recipe. When the boys were little, my mother, who was a funny lady, used to say, "Megan, your boys eat lamb chops like other boys eat lollipops!" My husband would then gather the bones from the boys' plates and suck on them. It's one of the few meals for which I allowed them to use their fingers.

MENU

Fennel Salad with Oranges
WINE / 2015 Pichot Vouray
(Loire Valley, France)

Rack of Lamb with Mustard Glaze
Roasted New Potatoes with
Fresh Rosemary
Peas with Prosciutto and
Fresh Mint
WINE / 2012 Ch. Deyrem-Valentin
Margaux (Bordeaux, France)

Lemon Olive Oil Cake with
Berry Coulis
WINE / 2014 Marcarini Moscato
d'Asti (Piedmont, Italy)

ENTERTAINING NOTES

3 DAYS BEFORE / Set table. Choose and purchase wine. Prepare playlist.

2 DAYS BEFORE / Food shop.

1 DAY BEFORE / Make Olive Oil Cake (don't put confectioners' sugar on until just about to serve). Make Berry Coulis if using. Peel garlic. Chop mint. Make mustard glaze.

DAY OF DINNER / Earlier in day make Fennel Salad with Oranges and put in refrigerator. Remove mustard glaze from refrigerator and keep out on counter. Clean peas if fresh; if fro-

zen, remove from freezer. Cut prosciutto. If you are using the Berry Coulis for the dessert, take out of refrigerator. 30 minutes before guests arrive take Rack of Lamb out of refrigerator and add glaze. Leave out on counter.

JUST BEFORE FAMILY AND GUESTS ARRIVE / Roast potatoes first as they can cool while making the Rack of Lamb. Put broiler on. You could have fennel salad preset at each place setting or just keep in large bowl to pass and serve family style. Prepare the rest of the dinner according to recipes.

PLAYLIST

Bonbon Era Istrefi / **Fast Car (Radio Edit)** Jonas Blue Dakota / **A Sky Full of Stars** Coldplay / **One Call Away (Remix)** Charlie Puth / **Inside Out** The Chainsmokers / **Tenerife Sea** Ed Sheeran / **High and Dry** Jamie Cullum, Geoff Gascoyne, and Sebastian de Krom / **Oblivion** Bastille / **Renegades** X Ambassadors / **Hero** Family of the Year / **Smooth Sailin'** Leon Bridges / **Speak Low (Bent Remix)** Billie Holiday / **Warwick Avenue** Duffy / **Who You Love** John Mayer and Katy Perry / **Under the Influence** Elle King / **Sing Sing Sing (RSL Remix)** Anita O'Day / **Stay With Me** Sam Smith / **No Diggity** Chet Faker / **Gimmer Some (Mike Mangini Remix)** Nina Simone / **Chocolate** The 1975 / **Sweetest Thing** U2 / **Pressure Off** Duran Duran and Janelle Monae

1 HOUR, 22 MINUTES; PLAYLIST AND SONGS AVAILABLE ON SPOTIFY (MEGANOBLOCK)

FENNEL SALAD WITH ORANGES

I learned this pretty-to-look-at and refreshing first course in a cooking class in Tuscany. My parents never cooked with fennel and at first I didn't like it but with the oranges in this recipe it really works nicely. If you have never tried fennel, please try this recipe.

Serves: 6 to 8

½ cup pine nuts
(or hazelnuts, optional)

3 fennel bulbs,
cored and thinly sliced
(about 5 cups). Save some
greenery from ends

2 oranges, zest and juice
(use Microplane)

2 oranges, peeled,
separated, and cut in pieces

½ cup olive oil
(more if necessary)

Kosher salt and
freshly ground pepper

Parmesan cheese, shaved
(use vegetable peeler)

1 Toast pine nuts in hot pan to golden. Set aside to cool.

2 Slice fennel and add to a large bowl. Grate zest of 2 oranges into bowl with fennel. Squeeze juice of those 2 oranges into a separate medium size bowl. Add the 2 peeled and cut-up oranges to large bowl with fennel.

3 In the medium bowl with the orange juice add the olive oil and combine. Pour this vinaigrette over fennel and oranges. Add toasted pine nuts.

4 Toss all ingredients together. Add more olive oil if necessary. Add salt and pepper to taste.

5 Sprinkle some chopped greenery from the tops of the fennel for decoration. If you like, add a little Parmesan cheese or have available for guests to add to their own bowls.

OPTIONAL: Could substitute hazelnuts. After toasting, chop roughly before adding to salad.

RACK OF LAMB WITH MUSTARD GLAZE

A John Dewar's classic. John Dewar's was a butcher shop that I went to for all of my meats for years until it closed. They would have bright yellow cards with recipes on the counter and I stumbled on this one day. I make it all the time; it's a family favorite. My friend Penny taught me a nifty trick to use while making it. Scrape the ends of your ribs with a sharp knife to remove any fat or bits of meat. This makes for a more attractive dish and ribs that are easier to hold in your hand.

This recipe is enough for two people. I find we can all eat about four per person and each rack comes with eight ribs so increase your amounts according to your number of guests.

Serves: 2

1 8-rib lamb rack

8 tablespoons olive oil

4 tablespoons Dijon mustard

2 tablespoons fresh Italian flat leaf parsley, chopped

4 tablespoons low sodium soy sauce

2 garlic cloves, crushed

Freshly ground pepper

1 Always take your meat out of the refrigerator 30 minutes before cooking. Preheat oven to broil.

2 FOR THE MUSTARD GLAZE: Whisk all ingredients except your meat together. Coat rack of lamb on both sides with half of the glaze.

3 Broil 5 minutes each side adding more glaze each time.

4 Turn oven from broil down to 400 degrees.

5 Bake for 10 to 15 minutes (for rare). Turn over halfway through. Add more glaze. Be careful not to make these too rare. I find if you are doing more than one rack in the oven, you need to adjust the time for this recipe. For instance, I made three racks one night. I broiled on one side for 10 minutes, turned over, broiled on the other side for just 5 minutes, and then turned oven from broil to 400 degrees and cooked another 10 minutes and they were perfect!

6 Remove from oven and let stand 5 minutes before carving.

ROASTED NEW POTATOES WITH FRESH ROSEMARY

The kitchen smells so fantastic when these are roasting in the oven. Obviously, if you prefer another herb you can substitute. Thyme is lovely with these as well. If you have leftovers, they are great the next day with eggs for breakfast.

Serves: 6

24 ounces new potatoes, scrubbed, cut in quarters

2 garlic cloves, peeled, left whole

2-3 sprigs fresh rosemary

6 tablespoons olive oil

Kosher salt and freshly ground pepper

1 Preheat oven to 375 degrees.

2 In a cast iron pan (if you have one, otherwise any ovenproof pan), place cut-up potatoes. Add garlic and rosemary branches. Add olive oil and toss. Add salt and pepper to taste and toss again.

3 Roast for approximately 45 minutes, stirring half-way through.

PEAS WITH PROSCUITTO AND FRESH MINT

This vegetable dish reminds me of spring. There is something about peas and lamb together that for me just works well. Some people might add butter to this dish but as you can see from my cooking, I prefer olive oil instead of butter. If you can find fresh peas, use them. Otherwise, frozen will do.

Serves: 8

---

2 garlic cloves,
   peeled, left whole

6 tablespoons olive oil

8 slices of prosciutto
   (or pancetta), chopped

2 pounds of fresh peas
   or 2 bags of frozen, thawed

4 tablespoons fresh mint,
   finely chopped

   Kosher salt and
   freshly ground pepper

1 In a sauce pan on medium heat, sauté garlic cloves in olive oil until golden, approximately 2 minutes. Add prosciutto and sauté approximately 1 minute. Add peas and stir.

2 Lower heat, cover pan, and cook another 5 to 8 minutes until peas are soft.

3 Just before serving, remove garlic cloves, add mint, and taste for seasoning. Prosciutto can be salty, so you may not need any salt. Drizzle a little bit of olive oil over peas just before serving.

LEMON OLIVE OIL CAKE WITH BERRY COULIS

This is a classic Italian dessert that I enjoy because it isn't super sweet. You can make this a day in advance, which even enhances the flavors. If I serve this for dinner, a guilty pleasure of mine is to have a piece for breakfast the next day with my coffee.

Serves: 8

CAKE

Olive oil (for pan)

Parchment paper

7 eggs, separated and at room temperature

1½ cups granulated sugar

1 cup olive oil

1 cup flour

3 tablespoons cornstarch

1½ teaspoons baking powder

Zest of 2 lemons (or orange if you prefer)

Confectioners' sugar (for sprinkling)

BERRY COULIS

4 cups (2 11-ounce boxes) blueberries or raspberries

½ cup water

1 tablespoon sugar (optional)

1 cinnamon stick

Juice of 1 lemon

1 You'll need a 10" spring form pan. Preheat oven to 350 degrees.

2 Spread olive oil on bottom and side of pan. Place cut piece of parchment paper on bottom and add more olive oil to top and sides. Set aside.

3 In a large bowl, whisk the egg yolks (separating the egg whites in another bowl) and gradually whisk in the granulated sugar and olive oil. In a separate medium bowl, combine the remaining dry ingredients. Add dry ingredients to the egg yolk mixture and combine.

4 In a separate bowl, beat egg whites with mixer on high speed until they form soft peaks. Fold half the whites into the yolk mixture then add rest until combined. Add grated lemon zest (or orange if you are using).

5 Transfer the batter to the prepared spring form pan. Bake cake for 30 to 40 minutes or until the top springs back when pressed with your fingertips.

6 Let cool approximately 10 minutes, then unlatch the spring and slide the cake onto a platter. Just before serving, sprinkle generously with confectioners' sugar and serve with berry coulis.

7 FOR BERRY COULIS: Combine all ingredients in a small pot and heat on medium for approximately 8 to 10 minutes. Turn off heat and let cool. Remove cinnamon stick. Place in blender until smooth. I make this once a week and pour on my yogurt or oatmeal in the morning. This is also lovely drizzled over ice cream.

COMMITTEE DINNER

» It can be fun to have committee meetings at someone's home instead of at the office, school, or museum. Since I enjoy cooking and entertaining, I'll often offer to host the meeting . I always find a cohesiveness to and camaraderie in sharing a meal—and drinking wine never hurts either! This menu I created as a celebratory dinner for having exceeded a goal for raising funds for the Museum of Fine Arts, Boston Fashion Council.

MENU

Asparagus over
Arugula Pesto

WINE / 2015 Elk Cove
Pinot Gris
(Willamette Valley, Oregon)

Veal Osso Buco
over Polenta

WINE / 2013 Jankara
Vermentino di Gallura
(Sardinia, Italy)

2010 Proprieta
Sperino Lessona
(Piedmont, Italy)

Chewy Chocolate
Orange Cookies

Chocolate Sorbet

WINE / 2010 Castello di Ama
VinSanto
(Tuscany, Italy)

ENTERTAINING NOTES

3 DAYS BEFORE / Set table. Choose and purchase wine. Prepare playlist.

2 DAYS BEFORE / Food shop (including meat) and buy flowers. Make Arugula Pesto. Make cookies.

1 DAY BEFORE / Make cookies and sorbet. Make Veal Osso Buco. Make sorbet.

DAY OF DINNER / Remove Veal Osso Buco from refrigerator and let stand to bring to room temperature. Cook asparagus and keep in refrigerator until ready to serve.

JUST BEFORE GUESTS ARRIVE / Assemble asparagus course and put out at place settings. Reheat Veal Osso Buco and make polenta or risotto.

PLAYLIST

Don't Stop the Music Rihanna / **The Very Thought of You** Nellie McKay / **Gonna Get Along Without You Now** She & Him / **Get Your Money Up** Keri Hilson, Keyshia Cole, and Trina / **Your Love** Nicki Minaj / **The Sweetest Taboo** Sade / **Enough Love** Duffy / **Video Games** Lana Del Rey / **High on a Mountain** Loretta Lynn / **Diamonds** Rihanna / **Bird Set Free** Sia / **Ex's & Oh's** Elle King / **Better When I'm Dancin'** Meghan Trainor / **No Regrets** Cecile McLorin Salvant and the Jean-Francois Bonnel Paris Quintet / **You Mean the World to Me** Toni Braxton / **My Guy** Mary Wells / **Girls Chase Boys** Ingrid Michaelson / **Bang Bang** Jessie J, Ariana Grande, and Nicki Minaj / **Harper Valley P.T.A.** Jeannie C. Riley / **Only Love** Andra Day / **My Love** Jess Glynne / **Roses** The Chainsmokers / **Wild Things** Alessia Cara / **Tom's Diner** Suzanne Vega / **99 Red Balloons** Nena / **What's Up?** 4 Non Blondes

1 HOUR, 28 MINUTES; PLAYLIST AND SONGS AVAILABLE ON SPOTIFY (MEGANOBLOCK)

ASPARAGUS OVER ARUGULA PESTO

I sometimes serve this as a first course for dinner parties. An easy, efficient, and attractive way to serve this dish is to preset it on your table at each plate just before guests sit down. This arugula pesto is also lovely as a spread on sandwiches and can be made in advance. If you like my Basil Pesto from the Super Bowl menu (page 50) or my Lemon Pesto from the Family Dinner menu (page 102) you can use either of those.

Serves: 6

ARUGULA PESTO

- 2 garlic cloves
- 1 cup pine nuts
- 8 cups arugula
- ½ cup olive oil
  (more if necessary for proper consistency)*
  Juice of 2 lemons
  Kosher salt and freshly ground pepper

ASPARAGUS

- Kosher salt
  (for boiling water)
- 2 bunches of asparagus, tough ends cut off (approximately 4 to 5 per person)
- 1-2 logs of goat cheese (or fresh mozzarella or ricotta if you prefer)
  A bunch of radishes, washed and thinly sliced (use a vegetable peeler)

1 FOR THE ARUGULA PESTO: Using a Cuisinart, pulse garlic and pine nuts until a dough forms. Add arugula and continue to pulse, using a spatula to clean sides of Cuisinart.

2 While machine is running, add olive oil to the top streamer. If you want a thinner consistency, add more olive oil. Squeeze in lemons. Pulse until blended.

3 Add salt and pepper to taste, only if necessary. Arugula has a very peppery taste, so you may not need to add any pepper at all. Notice that I do not add any Parmesan cheese to this recipe. I like to keep it light, but if you want, add some at the end to taste.

4 FOR THE ASPARAGUS: Boil water with some salt in a pot or a frying pan large enough to fit asparagus. Prepare an ice bath in a large bowl. Add asparagus to boiling water and cook until just tender, about 4 minutes depending on thickness of your asparagus. Test with a fork.

5 Using tongs, remove asparagus from the water and plunge into icy water, being careful not to break off ends. Drain asparagus and set aside to cool.

6 Spread pesto on the individual plates. Place asparagus on top of pesto and then the cheese on top of the asparagus.

7 Arrange some radish slices on top of the plate. Garnish with extra arugula leaves if you like. You can also serve this dish as a buffet item and place all of your asparagus on a platter instead of individual plates.

A NOTE ON OLIVE OIL

*I like to use a light olive oil when I'm making arugula pesto because arugula can have an intense flavor. Try an olive oil from Puglia.

VEAL OSSO BUCO OVER POLENTA

I served this for a winter committee dinner meeting and it was a huge hit. This recipe is fantastic for entertaining because you make it one or even two days in advance, then just gently reheat it for your guests. Serve over polenta or risotto.

Serves: 6

6	12-ounce veal shanks
	Kosher salt and freshly ground pepper
6-8	tablespoons of vegetable oil or olive oil
1	cup flour
4	carrots, peeled and sliced
2	celery stalks, sliced (including leaves on top)
½-1	onion (depending on size), diced
6	garlic cloves, sliced
2	cups red wine
4	cups veal or chicken stock
1	26-ounce box Pomi chopped tomatoes (or a can of chopped tomatoes)
4	sprigs fresh thyme
2	sprigs fresh rosemary
2	bay leaves
2	tablespoons fresh Italian flat leaf parsley, chopped (for serving)
2	tablespoons lemon zest (for serving)

1 Preheat oven to 350 degrees.

2 Season veal shanks liberally on both sides with salt and pepper. Leave out on counter for 30 minutes.

3 Add oil to a large ovenproof pot over medium heat. Meanwhile, dredge veal shanks in flour, shaking off excess. Brown the veal shanks a few at a time in the oil for about 5 minutes on each side, adding more oil if necessary. Don't crowd the veal shanks.

4 Remove from pan and keep shanks on a dish covered with foil. Add the carrots, celery, onion, and garlic to the pot and cook over medium heat for 2 to 3 minutes, stirring constantly.

5 Add wine, bring to a boil, and cook for 2 to 3 more minutes. Add stock, tomatoes, thyme, rosemary, and bay leaves. Return veal shanks to the pot, cover, and put in oven for 2 hours until the meat is really tender. Stir halfway through cooking time. Take pot out of oven to cool.

6 In the sink, strain the contents of the pot through a mesh strainer, with a large pot underneath. Place shanks on a dish. Remove the herbs. Take the strained vegetables and place in blender until smooth. Once blended, return to the pot with the gravy. Add the shanks back to the pot as well.

7 Cover and refrigerate overnight. Remove pot from refrigerator 2 hours before serving. If there is fat on the surface, skim it off.

8 Reheat the Osso Buco either on the stove, covered, over low heat or in 350 degree oven, covered, for approximately 30 to 45 minutes before serving. Serve over polenta or risotto. Sprinkle each serving with chopped parsley and lemon zest and serve with crusty Italian bread for dipping!

CHEWY CHOCOLATE ORANGE COOKIES

This is an old recipe that I got when my three sons took an art class as toddlers. At the start of class, the teacher and kids would make cookies and while they were baking the kids would paint, sculpt, and sing songs. Such lovely memories. These cookies became a family favorite and I love chocolate and orange together!

Makes: 4 dozen

1¾ cups flour (white or whole wheat)

¼ teaspoon baking soda

⅓ cup unsweetened cocoa powder

1 cup unsalted butter, softened

1 cup granulated sugar

½ cup dark brown sugar

1 teaspoon vanilla extract

1 egg

1 orange, zest plus juice of the orange

1 Preheat oven to 350 degrees.

2 Lightly grease baking sheets with butter or line them with parchment paper. Combine dry ingredients in a medium size bowl.

3 In a large mixing bowl, beat butter, the add sugar and brown sugar until combined. Add vanilla and egg, and beat some more. Add orange zest and orange juice and combine. Add dry ingredients to the butter mixture and combine.

4 Roll batter in your hands like meatballs, forming tablespoon-size mounds. Place onto prepared baking sheets leaving 2 inches between each cookie.

5 Bake approximately 8 minutes. You want them a little soft.

CHOCOLATE SORBET

This dessert is easy to make, with very few ingredients, and tastes like a Good Humor fudge pop. Of course, if you don't want to do all this work, by all means buy a nice quality sorbet or gelato and place in lovely bowls or martini glasses. This is one of those items where if a guest asks, "What can I bring?" you can easily say, "Thank you. It would be great if you could bring chocolate gelato."

Serves: 6

¾ cup sugar

¾ cup unsweetened cocoa powder

2 cups boiling water

1 teaspoon vanilla extract

1 You'll need an ice cream maker or 9" x 13" baking dish.

2 Combine sugar and unsweetened cocoa powder in a medium bowl. Slowly whisk in 2 cups boiling water until the sugar dissolves and the mixture is smooth. Stir in vanilla.

3 If you own an ice cream maker, cover bowl with plastic and put in refrigerator to cool for approximately 1 hour. After 1 hour, pour chocolate mixture in ice cream maker and let run for 25 minutes. Transfer frozen sorbet to an airtight container and place in freezer until firm, about 2 hours.

4 If you don't own an ice cream maker, place mixture in baking dish. Cover in plastic, then tin foil, and chill in freezer.

5 After 1 hour, when the mixture starts to freeze, use a fork to scrape it in the baking dish every 30 minutes or so for 2 hours. This makes a lovely granita, which is refreshing after a heavy meal.

6 Spoon into martini glasses atop plates and serve immediately, as the sorbet will turn watery fast. Place some cookies on the side.

SUMMER

HEART TO TABLE

FAMILY DINNER

» I put this menu together because many of the items can be made in advance. That way, I'm not in the kitchen all day on a beautiful summer day. The pesto and gravy can even be pulled from the freezer and heated up. Sometimes my sons arrive at different times on a Friday night in the summer so if I have pesto and gravy I can always make them a bowl of pasta if they want. The fish is easy to make and healthy. Everybody in my family likes green beans and the farm stands sometimes have them available in the summer. If the farm stand doesn't have green beans you can always substitute another green vegetable for this menu. My boys aren't big on dessert but when the strawberries are in season, I like having them cut up for them.

ENTERTAINING NOTES

3 DAYS BEFORE / Make Fuggedaboutit Tomato Gravy (or make even up to 1 month before and take out of freezer 1 day before dinner). Choose and purchase wines. Prepare playlist.

2 DAYS BEFORE / Buy ingredients for the Pesto only and make Pesto.

1 DAY BEFORE / Buy flowers if you need; otherwise, cut flowers from your garden the day of dinner. Make nuts

DAY OF DINNER / Go to farm stand and buy all ingredients fresh! Earlier in day you can macerate the strawberries. Cut green beans, peel garlic, and put in refrigerator. One hour before dinner, remove Pesto and Fuggedaboutit Tomato Gravy from refrigerator to bring to

room temperature. Could also take out tomatoes and peaches, as they will be nice and juicy. Set table outside if the weather is nice.

JUST BEFORE GUESTS ARRIVE / Assemble first course on plates. Preheat oven for cod or put grill on if using it. Sauté green beans. Put nuts out on kitchen counter or outside for guests to nibble on while you are preparing dinner.

PLAYLIST

Love Unlimited Blackbird Blackbird / **Yes I Do** Miles Bonny / **American Daydream** Electric Guest / **Get On The Good Foot** James Brown / **The High Road** Broken Bells / **Before The Dive** St. Lucia / **Happy Together** The Turtles / **Ballerina** George Benson / **Trip Teen Daze Remix** Vacationer / **My Number** Foals / **Low Rider** War / **Karate** Kennedy / **Don't Think Twice It's Alright** Waylon Jennings / **Give Me The Night** George Benson / **Just Fall in Love** Poolside / **Back to the Future (Part I)** D'Angelo / **After Midnight** J.J. Cale / **Hold On I'm Comin'** Sam & Dave / **Don't Worry Baby** The Beach Boys / **Let Her Go** Mac Demarco / **Til I Met Thee** Cody Chesnutt / **Think** Aretha Franklin / **Swim and Sleep (Like a Shark)** Unknown Mortal Orchestra / **Tropical Sun** Flume / **Security** Otis Redding / **Inspiration Information** Shuggie Otis / **The Fall** Rhye / **Zimbabwe** New Navy / **(Fallin' Like) Dominoes** Donald Byrd / **I Wonder** Rodriguez / **Bikes** Rubblebucket / **These Arms of Mine** Otis Redding / **Goodbye Weekend** Mac Demarco / **Learn to Fly** FKJ / **My Type** Saint Motel / **Carried Away** Passion Pit / **Another Life** D'Angelo

2 HOURS, 11 MINUTES; PLAYLIST AND SONGS AVAILABLE ON SPOTIFY (MEGANOBLOCK)

MENU

Roasted Mixed Nuts
with Rosemary

Peaches and Tomatoes
over Lemon Pesto

WINE / 2013 Punta
Crena Pigato 'Ca de Rena'
(Liguria, Italy)

Cod with Fuggedaboutit
Tomato Gravy

Green Beans
in Olive Oil and Garlic

WINE / 2013 Hirsch Vineyards
Bohan-Dillon Pinot Noir
(Sonoma, California)

Fresh Strawberries
Macerated in Sugar

WINE / 2015 Batasiolo Moscato
d'Asti (Piedmont, Italy)

ROASTED MIXED NUTS WITH ROSEMARY

Nuts are a very healthy snack. Here is a recipe for a good, easy, casual starter for people to eat while standing around in the kitchen talking. I also add these to my salads. You should experiment and see which herb you and your family and friends prefer. I grow lots of rosemary but they are lovely with sage, too. You can do one type of nut or two or even three types.

Serves: 10

3   cups unsalted nuts (try a combination of almonds, walnuts, and cashews)

½   cup fresh rosemary, chopped

3   tablespoons olive oil

Kosher salt (optional)

1 Preheat oven to 250 degrees.

2 Place tin foil or parchment paper on a rimmed baking sheet. (Helps to have no dishes to wash.)

3 On the baking sheet, add nuts, rosemary, olive oil, and a pinch of salt (if using). Using your hands or a spoon, stir until nuts are evenly coated.

4 Bake for 30 minutes, stirring halfway through cooking. Test for somewhat softened nuts that are golden in color. You may need 10 to 15 more minutes until they are roasted but not burned.

PEACHES AND TOMATOES OVER LEMON PESTO

This dish is gorgeous on a plate. I can guarantee your guests will be dazzled by it. In the summer when the peaches and tomatoes are so perfect, this is a lovely first course. If you like my Arugula Pesto from the Committee Dinner menu (page 88), you can substitute that. This recipe is almost identical to the Pesto in the Super Bowl Party menu (page 50) but in this summer version I reduce the garlic and increase the lemon, and leave out the Parmesan cheese.

Serves: 6

- 3 garlic cloves
- 1 cup pine nuts
- 8 cups basil
   (1 ounce of loose basil
   = 2 cups measured)
- 2 lemons, squeezed

   Kosher salt and
   freshly ground pepper
- ¼ cup olive oil
   (more if necessary for
   proper consistency)
- 6 peaches
- 6 tomatoes

1 Make pesto using instructions on page 50. This can be done a day or two in advance. Add a little olive oil on top and cover tightly. Keep in refrigerator.

2 Cut peaches and tomatoes into wedges just before guests arrive.

3 Pesto can turn dark so just before guests arrive spread pesto onto individual dishes. Place peaches and tomatoes on top of pesto, arranged in a circle. For decoration, you could lay a few basil leaves on the top center of each plate.

COD WITH FUGGEDABOUTIT TOMATO GRAVY

This is such an easy fish dish to make and it's healthy. Feel free to replace cod with any fresh white fish that is available to you. This is one of the recipes I use my Fuggedaboutit Tomato Gravy (page 20) for. I often just grab a quart out of the freezer whenever I need it. This could also be done on your outdoor grill in the summer months if you want to keep your kitchen cool.

Serves: 6

---

3 pounds fresh cod (or any other white fish)

1 quart of Fuggedaboutit Tomato Gravy

3 lemons, sliced

½ cup capers (optional)

Freshly ground pepper

Fresh Italian flat leaf parsley, chopped

1 You'll need a 9" x 13" baking dish. Preheat oven to 350 degrees.

2 Place fish in baking dish.

3 Cover fish with gravy. You may not need the whole quart—save some for other uses. Place sliced lemons on top. If using capers, add on top of lemons. Top with freshly ground pepper to taste. Cover tightly with tin foil and bake for 20 to 30 minutes.

4 Before serving, sprinkle fresh parsley on top and have extra lemons available for guests.

GREEN BEANS IN OLIVE OIL AND GARLIC

I grew up having this dish often. My mother wanted to be sure each of her six children ate fresh vegetables. If you liked greens beans, she would make you green beans but if another sibling didn't and he or she preferred carrots, my mother would make them carrots. When my parents divorced, she was going through the house to see what she wanted to take and she told me it struck her how in the kitchen cabinets there were so many small sauce pans. That was because she was such an amazing mother and even though she worked full time, she made the extra effort to be sure we each ate fresh vegetables. Interestingly enough, my husband's mother was the opposite. He told me that if he didn't finish his lima beans (can you imagine making a child eat lima beans?) he literally had to sit there all night until he did! Spooky!

Serves: 6

1 pound green beans, ends cut off

2 garlic cloves, peeled and left whole

½ cup water

¼ cup olive oil

Kosher salt and freshly ground pepper

1 Clean green beans and cut off ends.

2 Place beans and garlic in a sauce pan. Add water and cook on medium heat approximately 8 minutes. Don't overcook.

3 When most of the water has evaporated, add olive oil and cook 2 more minutes. Add salt and pepper to taste. Remove garlic cloves before serving.

4 You can also make green beans with my Fuggedaboutit Tomato Gravy (page 20). Just sauté green beans in some of the tomato gravy instead of the olive oil and garlic. It's delicious and tomatoes are so good for you.

FRESH STAWBERRIES MACERATED IN SUGAR

In the summer when the strawberries are in season they don't need much. As a matter of fact, I have stopped buying strawberries unless they are in season. During the fall and winter, I buy frozen strawberries to add to my smoothies.

Serves: 6

2 pints fresh strawberries, sliced

2 tablespoons confectioners' sugar

Zest of 1 orange (optional)

A splash of Grand Marnier (optional)

1 Clean strawberries and cut off tops. Slice strawberries and add sugar. Gently toss.

2 If you want to take this a little further, add to the bowl the zest of 1 orange peel using your Microplane (which, if you haven't bought one yet, do it now). Another fancy addition would be to add just a splash of Grand Marnier.

3 Refrigerate or leave out on counter to macerate and become juicy.

4 You could have fresh whipped cream, crème fraiche, or homemade vanilla ice cream available for guests but if the strawberries are in season you really don't need anything else. And since it is bathing suit season—who the hell needs the extra calories?!

MY BIRTHDAY PARTY

» Being with my family for my birthday makes me so happy. I sometimes get depressed on my birthday, as I really hate this aging thing...but if my boys are with me, I'm fine. In the summer, we eat outside every night. I use the grill all summer long. The tomatoes are so beautiful that you don't have to do much with them. The fish is fresh off the boat and I visit the farm stand each morning for vegetables. My husband is crazy about corn on the cob so as long as he'll shuck it, I'll make it for him. My sons know that I have to have a chocolate layer cake for my birthday. Just like my mother and my grandmother, we love our chocolate!

ENTERTAINING NOTES

3 DAYS BEFORE / Choose and purchase wines. Prepare playlist.

2 DAYS BEFORE / Set table if eating indoors. Buy flowers if you don't have in your own cutting garden.

1 DAY BEFORE / Make cake. Make Balsamic Syrup and store in tightly covered container.

DAY OF DINNER / Go to farm stand and buy all ingredients fresh! Go to your fishmonger and buy fish. Earlier in day you can shuck the corn and remove the kernels. You could clean and cut the veggies and herbs and put into a Ziploc bag (don't add olive oil until just before grilling). Make icing and ice cake. You could prepare the salad, but again don't add the vinaigrette until just before serving. Set table if eating outdoors. Cut flowers and put on table. You could grill peaches and vegetables earlier in day if you like and reheat in oven on 250 degrees for approximately 10 to 15 minutes before serving.

JUST BEFORE GUESTS ARRIVE / Turn on grill. Remove all vegetables and salad from refrigerator. Begin to prepare your fish and vegetables.

PLAYLIST

Even After All Finley Quaye / **Harvest Moon** Poolside / **Dreamin' Slow** Mac Demarco / **Coming Home** Leon Bridges / **Baby I'm Yours** Breakbot / **Early Orange** Blazo / **Simple Song** The Shins / **Born Too Late** Dent May / **70s 80s** Nightmares On Wax / **Any Major Dude Will Tell You** Steely Dan / **Take It Easy** Soulive / **She Can't Love You** Chemise / **Plastic Bubble** ALO / **Express Yourself** Lettuce / **Great Escape** Washed Out / **Lovers' Carvings** Bibio / **Can't Get Away** Rodriguez / **No Sugar Tonight/New Mother** The Guess Who / **Killing Switch** Last Lynx / **Southern Nights** Allen Toussaint / **Tears of Joy** Slow Club / **Over Your Shoulder** Chromeo / **Downright Stinson** Alex Bleeker & The Freaks / **Blossoms** Potatohead People / **Wait for the Moment** Vulfpeck / **Sun Go Down** Far Night / **Ghosts** On an On / **Mi Swing Es Topical** Quantic / **Swim Away** Furns / **Then Comes the Wonder** The Landing / **Soulful Strut** Young-Holt Unlimited / **Warm** Joey Pecoraro / **Back Up Train** Al Green / **Necessary Evil** Unknown Mortal Orchestra / **Take Me I'm Yours** Mary Clark

2 HOURS, 18 MINUTES; PLAYLIST AND SONGS AVAILABLE ON SPOTIFY (MEGANOBLOCK)

MENU

Bruschetta with
Tuscan White Bean Dip and
Slow-Roasted Tomatoes

WINE / Ruinart Champagne,
Blanc de Blanc (Reims, France)

Summer Salad

Grilled Halibut
Wrapped in Tin Foil with
Citrus and Herbs

Grilled Vegetables
with Balsamic Syrup

Fresh Sautéed Corn

WINE / 2006 Meursault-Charmes,
Domaine Des Comtes Lafon
(Meursault,France)

Chocolate Layer Cake with
Egg White Chocolate
Buttercream Frosting

WINE / 1960 Fonseca
Vintage Port (Douro, Portugal)

Grilled Peaches

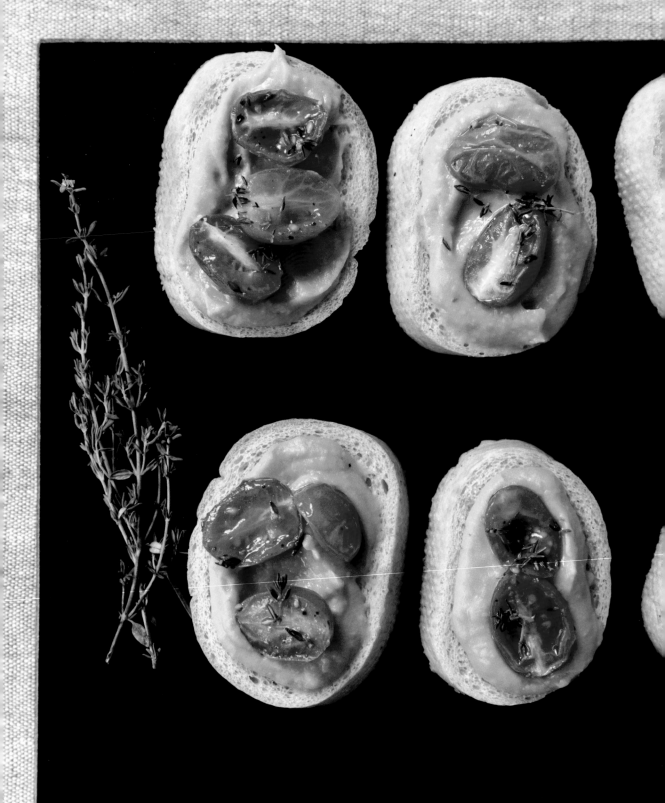

BRUSCHETTA WITH TUSCAN WHITE BEAN DIP AND SLOW-ROASTED TOMATOES

« There are endless possibilities for what you put on your bruschetta. My personal favorite is Slow-Roasted Tomatoes (page 58) on top of Pesto (page 50). Another favorite is a layer of Tuscan White Bean Dip (page 42) again with tomatoes on top.

Serves: 8

Italian bread

Olive oil

Pesto (or Tuscan White Bean Dip)

Slow-Roasted Tomatoes

1 Preheat oven to 350 degrees. You could also use an outdoor grill.

2 Slice Italian bread. Spread olive oil on both sides. Place on cookie sheet or directly on grill. Toast in oven or on grill for 1 minute, then turn and toast another minute.

3 Spread with Pesto (or Tuscan White Bean Dip) and spoon Slow-Roasted Tomatoes on top. Place back in oven or grill to heat approximately 2 minutes.

SUMMER SALAD

Every nationality has a summer salad. It's basically taking fresh tomatoes and cucumbers, adding fresh herbs, and tossing it all together in a vinaigrette. Depending on the nationality, the herbs can change. For instance, Russians use dill. Italians and Greeks love oregano. Try different herbs and see what you and your family like.

Serves: 6

6 tomatoes, cut into bite-sized pieces

6 cucumbers, peeled, seeds removed and quartered

½ red onion, chopped (optional)

2 tablespoons red or white wine vinegar

¼ cup olive oil

3 teaspoons fresh dill or fresh oregano

Kosher salt and freshly ground pepper

1 In a large bowl, combine tomatoes, cucumber, and onion (if using). Add vinegar and olive oil and toss.

2 Add chopped herbs. Season with salt and pepper to taste.

3 Toss again and watch this salad disappear!

GRILLED HALIBUT WRAPPED IN TIN FOIL WITH CITRUS AND HERBS

This is a dish I make in the summer months that my family and friends love. It's easy, healthy, and requires no dishes to clean afterwards.

Serves: 6

6 pieces halibut
(or any white fish),
for 3 pounds total
(½ pound each piece)

Olive oil

Kosher salt (optional)
and freshly ground pepper

3 lemons, sliced

2 oranges, sliced

3 limes, sliced

Fresh dill
(or any herb you like)

1 Tear 6 pieces of tin foil big enough to hold each piece of fish.

2 Pour some olive oil onto each and place fish on top of oil, coating both sides of fish. Sprinkle a tiny bit of salt (if using) and freshly ground pepper on each piece.

3 Place a few slices of each fruit on top (if you prefer, use just one form of citrus). Add chopped dill or whatever fresh herb you prefer.

4 Carefully fold tin foil around each piece, making sure it's tightly sealed.

5 Place packets directly onto hot grill for 10 minutes. No need to flip.

6 Serve on a platter and let guests choose their own foil packet and open themselves.

GRILLED VEGETABLES WITH BALSAMIC SYRUP

One summer, my sister-in-law gave me the best gift ever—a grill basket. I literally use it almost every night during the summer months. I cut up my vegetables into bite-sized pieces and grill them in the basket. I know that other people like cutting them lengthwise to get the grill marks, but I feel this is too time consuming. You don't need the Balsamic Syrup but you can make it available to guests if they want to pour onto their vegetables.

Serves: 6

GRILLED VEGETABLES

- 2 zucchini, cut into 1-2 inch pieces
- 1 white eggplant, peeled and cut into 1-2 inch pieces (if available, and if you like it)
- 2 red peppers, cut into 1-2 inch pieces
- 2 yellow peppers, cut into 1-2 inch pieces
- 2 orange peppers, cut into 1-2 inch pieces
- 2 tablespoons olive oil
- 3 tablespoons fresh herbs, chopped (rosemary, thyme, or marjoram)

  Kosher salt and freshly ground pepper

BALSAMIC SYRUP

- 1 cup balsamic vinegar (optional)

1 Heat grill on medium.

2 Use whatever vegetables look good that day: zucchini, eggplant, or whatever your family likes.

3 Place veggies in a Ziploc bag with all the other ingredients. Shake. Pour into grill basket and cook approximately 10 to 15 minutes, tossing occasionally until cooked to your liking—I don't like my vegetables too soft.

4 FOR THE BALSAMIC SYRUP: In a saucepan, cook balsamic vinegar on medium to high heat until it begins to thicken, approximately 10 to 15 minutes. Drizzle on top of vegetables before serving (or have available for guests to drizzle on their own plate).

FRESH SAUTEED CORN

Every summer, I look forward to going to the farm stand for fresh corn. My husband could eat it every night of the week if I let him. He shucks it and cuts it off the stalk for me. When I serve this for guests I usually estimate 1 or 2 ears per guest.

Serves: 6

6-10   ears fresh corn
on the cob

4   tablespoons
salted butter

Kosher salt and
freshly ground pepper

1 You'll need a cast iron or dark coated pan. (I bought some Starfrit pans, which are fantastic.)

2 Shuck corn and cut the kernels right off the cob into the pan. Add butter and sauté on medium heat for approximately 15 to 25 minutes, stirring often. Use a wooden spoon so you don't scratch your pan. You want to scrape up the brown bits that happen when the butter and sugar from the corn begin to caramelize.

3 Add salt and pepper to taste.

CHOCOLATE LAYER CAKE WITH EGG WHITE CHOCOLATE BUTTERCREAM ICING

Adapted from The Cake Bible *by Rose Bevy Beranbaum, Copyright 1988, William Morrow & Company, Inc. All Rights Reserved.*

For my birthday one summer, I received the book *The Cake Bible* from my good friend Susan. As you may be able to tell, I'm not a big baker, but I do love a chocolate layer birthday cake. One day as I was testing cake recipes, my son happened to be in the kitchen. He watched as I got frustrated and started to curse, which I often do while baking. He said, "Mom, you're not a baker." And he's right: I much prefer slicing, dicing, and sautéing to measuring vast amounts of sugar and flour. My mother, who made an extra buck by testing recipes in the '60s and early '70s, often used a Duncan Hines cake mix and added a delicious homemade butter icing. I did try two recipes from *The Cake Bible* and also two from *The Lily Wallace New American Cook Book* that my friend Theresa loaned me. After they flopped, I bought a Duncan Hines Dark Chocolate Fudge Cake Mix. If you like to bake, by all means make a cake from scratch but I use a cake mix and make my own icing.

Here is a killer icing, adapted from *The Cake Bible*. I put in ½ cup less sugar and reduced the butter by half. Can you imagine? The recipe called for 2 cups of butter—that's 4 sticks, folks....shoot me!

Serves: 8

3⅓ 3-ounce bars bittersweet chocolate for 10 ounces total, or approximately 2 cups of chopped chocolate* (60% or higher. Use chips if you can find them.)

1 cup unsalted butter, softened

4 large egg whites, at room temperature

1 cup sugar

A NOTE ON CHOCOLATE

*Use the best quality chocolate you can find. I've found that Valrhona, Callebaut, and Guittard are all good brands.

1 Break the chocolate into pieces and put in a double boiler over hot water to melt. (If you don't own a double boiler, put chocolate pieces in a bowl and place over boiling water in a pot.) Stir often. When melted remove from heat and let cool.

2 In a medium mixing bowl, beat the butter until smooth and creamy.

3 In another large mixing bowl, beat the egg whites until soft peaks form. Gradually add in sugar and continue to beat until stiff peaks form. Add the butter by the tablespoon to the egg white mixture. If the mixture looks slightly curdled, increase the speed a little and beat until smooth.

4 Add the melted, cooled chocolate all at once and beat until smooth. Spread on your layer cake. This icing can be made one day in advance and stored in an airtight bowl.

GRILLED PEACHES

In the summer, when the peaches are in season, I love to put them on the grill. I used to make peach ice cream but as I get older and worry about my weight I seem to make it less each summer. Maybe when I become a grandmother I'll go back to making homemade ice cream.

Serves: 6

6 fresh peaches, cut in half and stones removed

2 tablespoons olive oil

Kosher salt

1 Gently brush peaches with olive oil on both sides. Sprinkle some salt on top.

2 Grill approximately 5 to 6 minutes, turning over half-way through. You can eat these plain or drizzle some Balsamic Syrup (page 116) on top.

SPECIAL THANKS

I must begin by thanking my parents: my mother, for showing by example how to face any challenge with determination and grace; my father, who showed me that the kitchen is a place where you can be in control and be creative. Besides being out in nature, the kitchen is my favorite place to spend time.

For precious assistance from Maisa who provided constant encouragement, support, and hard work. Whenever she enters my kitchen and says, "Oh Megan, it smells delicious," that always brings a smile to my face. Thanks to Hobson as well for helping me serve guests with such class.

A warm thanks to Kristin Teig for her gorgeous photography and to Catrine Kelty for her brilliant food styling. The photo sessions were fun and I learned so much from these creative and talented women.

Having a vision of how I wanted this book to look was realized by the tremendous listening skills and vision of Robert Parsons of Seven Elm, the book designer. I couldn't be happier with the look of my new cookbook. With my pathetic computer skills, a big shout out goes to Andres Ribot for helping me organize this book and keeping me focused.

Big thanks to Carmine Martignetti of Martignetti Liquors and Len Presutti for their knowledgeable wine pairing suggestions. My humble thanks to Penny Matteson who shared many cookbooks with me and who should be writing her own.

With all of the dinner parties I threw this past year, sharing recipes with my family and friends, I have so many to thank for their words of encouragement and appreciation: Nancy Adams and Scott Schoen, Anne and Terrey Arcus, Chad Asnas, Cynthia and Tom Ballantyne, Terry Baybutt, Dan Benge, Mary Berghaus, Suzanne and Jeff

Bloomberg, Mary Boecker, Sarah Brown, Judy Bullitt, Allison Byrne, Matt Cambria, Pat and Dick Cavanagh, Nancie and Miceal Chamberlain, Linda Chernoff, Kathie Chrisicos, Don Clifford, Scottie Cochran, Jane Codman, Lucy and Steve Cookson, Lisa Craig, Jill and Cate Creevy, Jen Cristello, Victoria Croll, Lynn Dale and Frank Wisneicki, Kitty and Jerry Daly, Deb Dean, Carrie Doyle, Bill Drake, Leslie and Paul Durgin, Charbel El Hage, Rene Feuerman, Michele and Dan Finamore, Laura Finn, Ruthanne Fuller, Brett Gaede, Lydia Gilbert, Amie and John Hadden, Ronnie Harrington, Perry Heard, Veronica Heath, Simon Holmes, Kaley Jacobs, Bev and Mike Kazickas, Laura Kornhauser, Mona Kumar, Tina and Norman Lang, Taina Lyons, Debbie and John Mackall, Laurie McFarlane, Beth Martignetti, Debbie Miller, Donald Miller, Muff and Peter Morse, Maria Muller, Hannah Nead, Liz and Tom Niedermeyer, Anne and Jack Nordeman, Ashley and Alex Norton, Marjorie O'Malley, Anne and Juan Ocampo, Jeryl and Steve Oristaglio, Richard Ortner, Panos Panay, Pam Parmal and Bill Van Siclen, Brendan Richards, Tracy, Olivia, Sophie and Harlan Rieur, Karen Rodgers, Paul Roe, Karen Rotenberg, Sue Segar, Danilla, Mia and Tony Sessa, Lauren Shareshian, Irene and Ed Shaw, Pam and Jarvis Slade, Louisa and Nulsen Smith, Greg Star, Emily and Mark Stoehrer, Diane Suda, Amy, Katie, Annie Thind, Kerry Titheradge, Susan and Andrew Todres, Annie Vick, Barbara and Ingo Vogelsang, Lisa and Jeff Volling, Martha and Mark Volpe, Cheryl Wakeham, Tristana Waltz and Grier Eliasek, Anna and Spencer Waresk, Lauren Whitley, Dana Wilson, Emi Winterer, Joan and Al Zagami, Lucinda Zuniga. If I have left anyone out I sincerely apologize.

I need to thank my siblings, Johnnie, Kitten, Hellie, Cassie, and Jason who suggested some hysterical and ridiculous titles for this book which didn't make the cut such as: *From Jersey with Love: Meals You Can't Fuggedaboutit*, *Going Jersey: Delish and Easy to Make Meals*, and the best one of all, *Megan Magoo's Guinea Bastard Cookbook*! Warm thanks to the Spreitzers— Maggie, Brennan, Linda and Andy—for title suggestions, music, and endless inspiration.

A warm thanks to my three sons, Kevin, Gregory, and Rob who always encourage me to reach my goals while making me laugh at myself!

And finally, my husband, who is footing the bill. God, I hope I at least break even...

RAVES

"What an extraordinary evening at your home this week! You were the ideal "convener" for the first-ever event bringing together members of our two Boards of Trustees. Truth to tell, we were all a bit anxious, but your amazing hospitality turned what could have been an awkward evening into a real catalyst for future collaboration! The food was fantastic, the music was elevating, and the atmosphere you created was—perfect! Sincerest thanks to you and Robert, from us all." —*Richard Ortner, President of The Boston Conservatory at Berklee College of Music*

"Thank you for a perfect Sunday afternoon. My favorite day of the week for something special and out-of-the-ordinary. There is nothing like being your guinea pigs! Actually, you could pay me to do it and make a little extra on the side. And as always you cared for us with your Megan grace and fun and elegance. Thank you for a nifty day." —*Vicki*

"Thanks for the delicious stew and 'to die for' cookies." —*Deb*

"I want to thank you again. We had a great time, the food was delicious, I give it a 5-star and Italian thumbs up." —*Al and Joan*

"Thank you so much for including Scott and me at your most delicious Italian buffet! Every dish was beautifully presented and so yummy! We love Italian food and we both agreed that your dishes, friends, and home are at the top of our dining experiences! Thank you for including us!!" —*Nancy*

"It was a lovely evening. The backdrop of your lovely home, hospitality, and restaurant-style dining always make it feel extra special!" —*Lisa*

"It was a fine supper—good people, good conversation, and outstanding food. I plan to try some of those recipes on my family and I don't expect leftovers. Thanks for the invite." —*Donald*

"The osso bucco was to die for!! I can't wait to try the recipes. Thank you again for a wonderful evening at your beautiful home. The meal was absolute perfection right down to the music playlist. I LOVED it! Can't wait for your cookbook to be published." —*Emi*

"Thanks, Megan, for the lovely springtime gathering. The recipes for the scrumptious fare did not include your secret ingredient for success: gracious hostessing and loving spirit!" —*Diane*

"Thank you so much for such a lovely lunch. The company was engaging and relaxing. All of the food was over the top amazing but that lemon cake with the blueberry sauce made my week!!" —*Rene*

"Thank you so so much for an epic weekend! I love spending time with your beautiful family and feeling all the LOVE! Such a treat. Your devotion to your family definitely spills over to your guests! Another wonderful East Hampton weekend of Diamonds Dishes, family love, and fun in the sun for the books!" —*Kaley*

"Jerry and I feel so fortunate to be on your list of friends. The 'Italian buffet' taste testing was a visual and culinary feast. And it was amazingly delicious! Thank you! The room was filled with people saying 'yum,' great conversations, and laughter. Many thanks to you both for a wonderfully fun gathering and always for being so welcoming. Sending you lots of fun & success in launching your next book...When will we be able to buy an autographed copy?" —*Kitty and Jerry*

"Thanks for including me in the Sunday feast! Wonderful event—food, hospitality, company." —*Dick*

"Thank you for hosting the most delicious and warm Super Bowl Sunday ever. Your passion for food, family, and friends is so obvious and you do it beautifully. Thank you again for having us" —*Lynn and Frank*

Published by
Diamonds Dishes
Chestnut Hill, MA 02467

For information about ordering,
please contact Diamonds Dishes,
info@diamondsdishes.com

Printed by
The Studley Press
151 East Housatonic Street
Dalton, MA 01226

Photographs by
Kristin Teig

Food Styling by
Catrine Kelty

Book Design by
Robert Parsons / Seven Elm

Visit Diamonds Dishes at
www.diamondsdishes.com

Visit Megan on the web at
www.meganoblock.com

ISBN: 978-1-5323-1879-5